UNLOCKING THE OLD TESTAMENT

UNLOCKING THE OLD TESTAMENT

VICTOR L. LUDLOW

Deseret Book Company
Salt Lake City, Utah
1981

©1981 Deseret Book Company
All rights reserved
Printed in the United States of America
First printing August 1981
Library of Congress Catalog Card Number 81-68266
ISBN 0-87747-873-2

Contents

Preface	*vii*
Key to Abbreviations	*ix*
Introduction	1
Genesis	3
Exodus	22
Leviticus	32
Numbers	41
Deuteronomy	51
Joshua	54
Judges	62
Ruth	74
The Books of Samuel	76
The Books of Kings	82
The Books of Chronicles	110
Ezra and Nehemiah	114
Esther	117
Job	118
Psalms	125
Proverbs	138
Ecclesiastes	140
The Song of Solomon	142
Isaiah	145
Jeremiah	177
Lamentations	187

Ezekiel   190
Daniel   194
Hosea   196
Joel   200
Amos   208
Obadiah   210
Jonah   212
Micah   215
Nahum   220
Habakkuk   222
Zephaniah   224
Haggai   226
Zechariah   228
Malachi   231
Bibliography   234
Index   235

Preface

Many reasons could be given as to why the Old Testament is the least read and least understood book of the standard works: the Old Testament writers lived thousands of years ago, they wrote in Hebrew and used unfamiliar poetic styles, their culture and symbolism are alien to us, and so on. These barriers are gradually overcome as one reads the Old Testament while studying other scriptures, commentaries, and supplementary resources. As the reader appreciates the great variety and richness of the Old Testament writings, he can choose the books, chapters, and sections that will best enlighten and inspire him at a particular time. This book should encourage and help in that selection process, as it provides introductions and background material for each of the thirty-nine Old Testament books.

While reading the Old Testament, most readers have questions about certain passages and topics. Answers to some commonly asked questions are included in this book.

Charts, maps, illustrations, and extra enrichment material about the Old Testament are also provided.

Together, these introductions, answers to commonly asked questions, and additional materials will help overcome some of the barriers that often discourage the Old Testament reader. However, this book will only prove helpful if the reader will exert effort in reading and studying the scriptures and other available material.

The purpose of this book is not to answer every question or even most questions that an Old Testament reader might have. It does, however, attempt to lead the reader into the work and through some of the more difficult passages. It suggests other resources, especially those found in the new Latter-day Saint edition of the King James Version of the Bible. References in this book to the Topical Guide, Bible Dictionary, Joseph Smith Translation, and Maps pertain to that edition of the Bible. (The abbreviation "BD" refers to the Bible Dictionary. "TG" refers to the Topical Guide. "JST" refers to the Joseph Smith Translation.)

With thanks to my father, Daniel, for his example; my wife, V-Ann, for her patience; our six children for their long-suffering; and Charlotte, Julie, Lorraine, and Susan for their help.

Key to Abbreviations

AF   *Articles of Faith,* James E. Talmage
AGQ   *Answers to Gospel Questions,* Joseph Fielding Smith
DS   *Doctrines of Salvation,* Joseph Fielding Smith
FPM   *Faith Precedes the Miracle,* Spencer W. Kimball
HC   *History of the Church,* Joseph Smith
JD   *Journal of Discourses*
MD   *Mormon Doctrine,* Bruce R. McConkie
MFP   *Messages of the First Presidency,* compiled by James R.
        Clark
MOD   *Man: His Origin and Destiny,* Joseph Fielding Smith
PGPC   *Pearl of Great Price Commentary,* Milton R. Hunter
TPJS   *Teachings of the Prophet Joseph Smith,* compiled by
        Joseph Fielding Smith

Introduction

The Old Testament is a collection of books, including histories, genealogies, laws, biographies, dramas, poems, proverbs, hymns, and prophecies. It might be compared to a Latter-day Saint library collection of the following works: histories of the Church's settlements from New York to Utah, genealogies of the handcart company descendants, missionary handbooks and directives outlining missionaries' duties and obligations, biographies of the Church presidents, scripts from the Hill Cumorah and Promised Valley productions, selected poems and "Mormonisms" from Church periodicals, the LDS hymnbook, and a large sampling of general conference addresses.

Such resources are familiar to most Latter-day Saints, but some background material and explanations would have to be given to non–Latter-day Saints before they could understand and appreciate this literature.

Members of the Church are in much the same position with the Old Testament. They need information about the background, purposes, and difficult passages of each book of the Old Testament to help them unlock the spiritual treasures in this magnificent volume of ancient scripture.

The following chart illustrates the variety of Old Testament books.

The Old Testament, an Ancient Library

Types of records	*Collections*	*Books*	
History (world, national, and family) Genealogy Law (religious and commercial)	The Pentateuch	Genesis Exodus Leviticus Numbers Deuteronomy	
History Biography (judges, kings, prophets, and common people)	History	Joshua Judges Ruth 1 and 2 Samuel 1 and 2 Kings	1 and 2 Chronicles Ezra Nehemiah Esther
Poetry Hymns Proverbs Drama Ballads	Poetry and Wisdom	Job Psalms Proverbs	Ecclesiastes Song of Solomon
Prophecy Poetry History Biography	The Prophets	Isaiah Jeremiah Lamentations Ezekiel Daniel Hosea Joel Amos Obadiah	Jonah Micah Nahum Habakkuk Zephaniah Haggai Zechariah Malachi

The reader should study the following items in the Bible Dictionary to better understand the Old Testament as a whole: Scripture, Bible, Canon, Italics, Joseph Smith Translation, Writing, Scroll, Roll, Codex, Lost Books, Apocrypha, Pseudepigrapha, Hagiographa, Masoretic Text, Septuagint, Vulgate, Dead Sea Scrolls, Tell el-Amarna Letters, Talmud.

Genesis

Genesis contains the religious history of four gospel dispensations spread over two and one-half thousand years. The first eleven chapters briefly review the dispensations of Adam, Enoch, and Noah. The remaining thirty-nine chapters evaluate the dispensation of Abraham through the four generations of Abraham, Isaac, Jacob, and Joseph.

Often called the "First Book of Moses," this record was first written by Moses, the prophet of the fifth dispensation. In reviewing the earlier religious history of the earth, Moses not only had access to oral traditions and possibly written records, but he also had seen these earlier events in a divine vision. (Moses 1:4, 8, 27-35, 40-41.) Selecting from his vast knowledge of the past, he presented a brief overview of the genesis (origin) of the earth and its earliest dispensations. Then he discussed the dispensation of Abraham in more depth and highlighted the personalities of the great patriarchs. He also gave examples of their humanness and personal challenges. He told of family members (usually the elder sons) and how they sometimes sinned and lost the blessings of the birthright. He concluded the book with the promises given to the sons of Israel and their descendants who would continue to live in Egypt after the deaths of Jacob and Joseph.

In Genesis, Moses presented the good and the bad, the righteous prophets and the devil worshipers. He identified a God of love and mercy, who created the earth and blessed it for the growth and protection of his righteous children, and also a God of indignation and justice, who allowed plagues and wars to punish his wicked offspring. In the context of Moses' involvement with the Israelites in the wilderness, one can see why Moses selected and stressed these themes rather than a detailed account of the creation, a complete history of earlier time periods, or more events from earlier dispensations. His purpose was to show God's work with his children.

Bible Dictionary references:

1. Creation and Adam (1-3): Genesis; Firmament; Garden of Eden; Adam; Eve; Flesh; Devil; Heaven; Spirit; Fall of Adam; Cherubim; Prayer; Angels; Marriage; Family; Abel; Cain.
2. Enoch and Noah (4-10): Dispensations; Genealogy; Enoch; Zion; Giants; Noah; Cubit; Rainbow; Ham; Arabia; Aram.
3. Abraham (11-23): Babylon; Abraham; Abraham, Covenant of; Haran (person and place); Hebrew; Patriarch; Melchizedek; Melchizedek Priesthood; Tithe; Firstborn; Esau; Circumcision; Hospitality; Ammon.
4. Isaac and Jacob (24-38): Isaac; Jacob; Birthright; Israel; Levirate Marriage.
5. Joseph (39-50): Joseph; Egypt; Pharaoh; Embalming; Shiloh.

How Long Were the "Days" of Creation?
(Gen. 1:5)

Three theories are accepted by various Latter-day Saints as a possible answer to this question:

1. One day equals one day.

Some hold that each day of the creation was the same length as under our present system of time. They believe that if man, with his limited capacity, experience, and power can use greenhouses and controlled conditions to put "years" of growth on young trees within a few weeks, then God, with his capacities, could develop this earth through the seven periods of creation within a week of our time.

2. One day equals one thousand years.

Many Latter-day Saints combine the creation stories of Genesis and the Pearl of Great Price with a vision given to Abraham wherein he was told that one revolution of the Lord's governing star, Kolob, was equal to one thousand years of earth's time. (Abr. 3:4.) They suppose that this same time relationship existed before the days of Abraham and before the fall of Adam (and of the earth) and that each "day" of creation (according to Kolob time) was a thousand years of our time. Based upon the first viewpoint discussed (one day equals one day), if God has the power to complete a creation stage within one day, he could also do it within one thousand years.

3. One day equals one time (of any length).

Some Latter-day Saints combine the various creation accounts and note that Abraham used the word "time," not "day," to summarize the events of each creative period. They also stress that only after each stage or series of creative events was completed was it called a "day" or a "time." Thus, each period would not even have to be the same length of time, but when one stage of the creation was completed it was called a "day" and then the next stage was begun. (See Abr. 4:5, 8, 13, 19, 23, 31; 5:2-3, 13.) The name "day" or "time" was only given the work after it was completed. The term "day" would thus not have to be a set length of time. It could be like our use of the term "day" in the statement, "We live in a modern *day* and age." Here "day" means the last number of years (even centuries) of our time.

Some adherents of this third viewpoint also suggest that geologists, earth scientists, and other specialists usually recognize the same general sequence of events as recorded in the creation story, but identify many thousands and millions of years for each stage.

Summary:

The Lord has not revealed in the scriptures the exact length of time of the creation process. It is important to note what questions of the creation he did answer. He did not tell us how long the creation took, but he did emphasize *who* created this earth—God, and *why*—for man and woman so that they could achieve their immortality and eternal life. Eventually we will know the answers to the questions of the creation, but for now it is important to recognize who the creator was and why he organized this earth and allowed us to come here.

Was Adam "Created" or "Born"?
(Gen. 1:26-27)

Adam was created from the dust (or elements) of the earth. We also are made from these elements. Within a mother's womb the elements of the original cells are joined by other earthly components until a developed baby is born. Adam was "born into the world by water, and blood, and the spirit, which [God had] made, and so became of dust a living soul." (Moses 6:59.)

The prophets Joseph Smith, Brigham Young, and Joseph Fielding Smith taught that Adam was created by the same natural means as we were created. (See HC 6:476; JD 7:285-86; 11:122; MOD, pp. 276-77; DS 1:139-40.)

For example, Brigham Young stated:

I believe that the declaration made in these two scriptures is literally true. God has made His children like Himself to stand erect, and has endowed them with intelligence and power and dominion over all His works, and given them the same attributes which He Himself possesses. He created man, as we create our children; for there is no other process of creation in heaven, on the earth, in the earth, or under the earth, or in all the eternities, that is, that were, or that ever will be. . . . There exist fixed laws and regulations by which the elements are fashioned to fulfill their destiny in all the varied kingdoms and orders of creation, and this process of creation is from everlasting to everlasting. (JD 11:122.)

Joseph Fielding Smith and the First Presidency stated:

Adam, our progenitor, "the first man," was, like Christ, a pre-existent spirit, and like Christ he took upon him an appropriate body, the body of a man, and so became a "living soul." The doctrine of the pre-existence,—revealed so plainly, particularly in latter days, pours a wonderful flood of light upon the otherwise mysterious problem of man's origin. It shows that man, as a spirit, was begotten and born of heavenly parents, and reared to maturity in the eternal mansions of the Father, prior to coming upon the earth in a temporal body to undergo an experience in mortality. It teaches that all men existed in the spirit before any man existed in the flesh, and that all who have inhabited the earth since Adam have taken bodies and become souls in like manner.

It is held by some that Adam was not the first man upon this earth, and that the original human being was a development from lower orders of the animal creation. These, however, are the theories of men. The word of the Lord declares that Adam was "the first man of all men" (Moses 1:34), and we are therefore in duty bound to regard him as the primal parent of our race. It was shown to the brother of Jared that all men were created in the *beginning* after the image of God; and whether we take this to mean the spirit or the body, or both, it commits us to the same conclusion: Man began life as a human being, in the likeness of our heavenly Father.

True it is that the body of man enters upon its career as a tiny germ embryo, which becomes an infant, quickened at a certain stage by the spirit whose tabernacle it is, and the child, after being born, develops into a man. There is nothing in this, however, to indicate that the original man, the first of our race, began life as anything less than a man, or less than the human germ or embryo that becomes a man. (MFP 4:205.)

Creation of Woman
(Gen. 2:21-24)

Moses records that Eve was created from Adam's rib. According to a contemporary prophet, Bruce R. McConkie, this Mosaic account is merely figurative and Eve was placed on the earth in the same manner as was Adam. (MD, p. 242; see also commentary on Gen. 1:26-27 in this book, and JD 7:285.)

Eve coming from the rib of Adam is considered symbolic of her role as a companion to the man. She is to stand at the side of man to be the joint-inheritor with him in receiving a celestial reward. They would also become one flesh and one in purpose during this life and the eternities because of their everlasting covenant of marriage. (DS 2:72; see also PGPC, pp. 145-46.)

Death on the Day Adam Partook of the Forbidden Fruit
(Gen. 3:3-5)

Adam did experience death on the day he partook of the forbidden fruit. He actually experienced two deaths, each within its own time framework of a day.

The first death occurred on that day of the earth's time system. The death was spiritual, as Adam was cut off from the presence of the Lord. (See D&C 29:41.)

One of the Lord's days is as one thousand of our years. (See Abr. 3:4.) On that day (or time) of the Lord, Adam died physically. He did not live longer than one thousand years. (See Abr. 5:13 and Gen. 5:5.) His 930 years upon the earth were not even a day of the Lord's time.

Enmity
(Gen. 3:15)

Enmity is a feeling of innate dislike. For example, most people dislike snakes, even though they may never have had a life-threatening encounter with a snake.

The Lord has placed enmity between mortals and Satan. However, individuals can lose this fear of the arch-enemy if they follow his encouragements and temptations. Before they know it, they become all too familiar with Satan as they come under his bonds and buffetings. However, the righteous maintain a distrust and hostility toward the devil and never become familiar with him. Their enmity toward him along with the Lord's protection guarantees that he will never have power to tempt them beyond their means to withstand. (See TG "Tempt" and "Temptation.")

Cain's Offering
(Gen. 4:3-7)

See Moses 5:18-26. Cain followed and obeyed Satan's command when he brought his offerings to the Lord. Yet he still could have been accepted and blessed by God if he had obeyed the Lord. (See BD "Cain" and TPJS, pp. 58, 169.)

Merciful Reasons for the Flood
(Gen. 6:17)

The Bible reader often considers God's reason for the flood as severe judgment upon the wicked. However, there are many reasons why a merciful Heavenly Father would have sent a flood. Among these are the following:

1. The wicked would have less time in this phase of their existence to commit further sins.
2. God's prophets had already demonstrated his power and witnessed his judgments; to have allowed more witnesses would have brought the people under greater accountability.
3. God's spirit children still residing in his presence needed a more pure spiritual environment in which to come.
4. The earth itself was a living entity and desired a rest from wickedness. (See Moses 7:48.)
5. The earth needed to go through its own baptism of water preparatory for a later baptism of fire and eventual celestialization. (See TG "Earth, Cleansing of.")

John Taylor said:

Now I will go back to show you how the Lord operates. He destroyed a whole world at one time save a few, whom he preserved for his own special purpose. And why? He had more than one reason for doing so. This antediluvian people were not only very wicked themselves, but having the power to propagate their species, they transmitted their unrighteous natures and desires to their children, and brought them up to indulge in their own wicked practices. And the spirits that dwelt in the eternal worlds knew this, and they knew very well that to be born of such parentage would entail upon themselves an infinite amount of trouble, misery and sin. And supposing ourselves to be of the number of unborn spirits, would it not be fair to presume that we would appeal to the Lord, crying, "Father, do you not behold the condition of this people, how corrupt and wicked they are?" Yes. "Is it then just that we who are now pure should take of such bodies and thus subject ourselves to most bitter experiences before we can be redeemed, according to the plan of salvation?" "No," the Father would say, "it is not in keeping with my justice." Well, what will you do in the matter; man has his free agency and cannot be coerced, and while he lives he has the power of perpetuating his species?" I will first send them my word, offering them deliverance from sin, and warning them of my justice, which shall certainly overtake them if they reject it, and I will destroy them from off the face of the earth, thus preventing their increase, and I will raise up another seed." Well, they did reject the preaching of Noah, the servant of God, who was sent to them, and consequently the Lord caused the rains of heaven to descend incessantly for forty days and nights, which flooded the land, and there being no means of escape, save for the eight souls who were obedient to the message, all the others were drowned. But, says the caviller, is it right that a just God should sweep off so many people? Is that in accordance with mercy? Yes, it was just to those spirits that had not received their bodies, and it was just and merciful too to those people guilty of the iniquity. Why? Because by taking away their earthly existence he prevented them from entailing their sins upon their posterity and degenerating them, and also prevented them from committing further acts of wickedness. (JD 19:158-59.)

Seven Pairs and One Pair of Animals
(Gen. 7:2)

Moses recorded that Noah took one pair of most animals, but that he took seven pairs of the "clean" animals. These would be clean animals according to Moses' definition. (See Lev. 11.)

These domesticated animals would be necessary for Noah's family to provide sacrifices and sustenance after the flood, and yet they would also become a prey to the wild animals released after the ark was opened. The larger numbers of these "clean" animals would provide food for both man and beast.

Also, the number seven was symbolic of wholeness. This number showed up repeatedly in Noah's episode—he not only collected seven pairs of clean animals, but he had seven days to load the ark, it floated seven months before it rested on Mount Ararat, and Noah waited seven days between each time he released a bird.

Should We Include Meat in Our Diets?
(Gen. 9:2-5)

After the flood, the Lord told Noah that all living animals could be used as food. Noah was not commanded to eat meat, but if he did, he was to respect the lives of the animals and not kill them wantonly.

Joseph Fielding Smith commented:

The inference in this interpretation is that the use of the flesh of living creatures should be indulged in sparingly although there was no sin in the shedding of their blood when required for food. There is no inference in the scriptures that it is the privilege of men to slay birds or beasts or to catch fish wantonly. The Lord gave life to every creature, both the birds in the heavens, beasts on the earth, and the fishes in the streams or seas. They also were commanded to be fruitful and multiply and fill the earth. It was intended that all creatures should be happy in their several elements. Therefore to take the life of these creatures wantonly is a sin before the Lord. (AGQ 4:43-44.)

Why Is Blood Not to Be Eaten?
(Gen. 9:4)
Joseph Fielding Smith gave the following answer:

The blood plays a far more important part in this mortal world, whether it is the blood of human beings or the blood of other creatures, than is generally understood. It is the life-giving fluid of the mortal body; but it has in it the seeds of death as well as the sustaining power of mortal life. Its duties are many and varied, but it is not the purpose here to recount them. Notwithstanding its great importance to the physical body, it is, above all else, a mortal element. (AGQ 3:100.)

How and Why Was the Earth Divided?
(Gen. 10:25)
Some scholars believe the earth was divided socially and politically into different nations and tribes.

The more common explanation is that the land masses of the earth were physically divided into continents.

The reason for the earth's division is found in the story of the Jaredites (Ether 1) and in the following quotation from President John Taylor:

In the days of Peleg the Lord divided the earth, hence the eastern and western hemisphere, doubtless thinking by doing so he would have a better opportunity to preserve some of the human family from going down to perdition. But still the devil found ready access to the hearts of the people generally, and many became so corrupt that God had to destroy them. But before allowing his justice to overtake them, he saved unto himself certain good seed and planted it in different parts of his vineyard. (JD 18:331.)

(See TG "Earth, Dividing of.")

Chronology of Abraham
(Gen. 11:27–25:10)
Age Event (and Scriptural References)
Birth about 2000 B.C. (Gen. 11:26.)

? Sought for holy priesthood; attempt was made to offer him as a human sacrifice in Ur. (Abr. 1:1-27.)

? Famine in the land; Abram's written records; his brother, Haran, dies. (Abr. 1:28-31; Gen. 11:27-28.)

? Abram marries Sarai, daughter of Haran. (Abr. 2:2.)

? Abram and Lot with wives (and father, Terah, following) move to Haran. (Abr. 2:3-5; Gen. 11:29-31.)

? Abram and Lot pray; Abram given blessing and priesthood. (Abr. 2:6-11.)

62 Abram sixty-two years old when he leaves Haran. (Abr. 2:14-15.)

? Abram and group go to Jershon (in Syria?) and Abram prays that famine would be turned from his father's house. (Abr. 2:16-17.)

75 Terah dies (Abram apparently at burial); Abram leaves homeland and kindred to go to Canaan. (Gen. 11:32; 12:1-5.)

? Abram goes through Canaan; famine in land; travels to Egypt. (Abr. 2:18-21; Gen. 12:6-10.)

? Sarai introduced as his sister. (Abr. 2:22-25; Gen. 12:11-13.)

? Abram's knowledge of stars, creation, and so on received through revelation and the Urim and Thummim. (Abr. 3:1-28; 4:1-31; 5:1-21.)

? Episodes with Abram and Sarai in Egypt. (Gen. 12:14-20.)

? Return to Bethel, Canaan, and separation from Lot. (Gen. 13:1-13.)

? Abram promised Canaan as inheritance; he dwells in Hebron. (Gen. 13:14-18.)

? He rescues Lot. (Gen. 14:1-16.)

? Abram and Melchizedek. (Gen. 14:17-24; D&C 84: 14; Alma 13.)

? Abram's vision with divided animals. (Gen. 15:1-21.)

86 Hagar as second wife; she conceives and bears Ishmael. (Gen. 16.)

99 Abram receives new name of Abraham; covenant of circumcision; Isaac's birth promised. (Gen. 17.)

99 Three divine messengers; bargaining about the righteous in Sodom. (Gen. 18.)

99 Destruction of Sodom and Gomorrah; Lot and two daughters preserved. (Gen. 19.)

99 Abraham, Sarah, and Abimelech. (Gen. 20.)

100 Son Isaac born; several years later Hagar and Ishmael leave. (Gen. 21.)

c. 115 Test of faith for Abraham and Isaac. (Gen. 22.)

137 Sarah dies; Abraham purchases burial ground in Hebron. (Gen. 23; see 17:17.)

140 Finds a wife, Rebekah, for Isaac. (Gen. 24; 25:20.)

c. 140 Abraham takes a third wife, Keturah, and has six more sons; gives them their inheritances. (Gen. 25:1-6.)

160 Isaac and Rebekah have twins. (Gen. 25:14-34.)

175 Abraham dies and is buried at Hebron. (Gen. 25:7-10.)

Abraham's Travels
(Gen. 12:1)
See Map 2 in the LDS edition of the Bible.

Five City-States near the Dead Sea
(Gen. 14:2, 8)
Genesis 14 records how Abraham rescued Lot, his family, and other captives who were taken from five city-states

in the plains near the Dead Sea. Two of these cities, Sodom and Gomorrah, are well known, while the other three, Admah, Zeboiim, and Zoar, are less familiar.

The story has puzzled scholars, but the exact order of names, the awkward style, and the unusual events of this chapter point to an authentic, ancient record that must have been familiar to Moses. In the 1970s an archaeological site in Syria was excavated that helps us understand more of this patriarchal time period. The site is known as Ebla, and includes a library of almost 20,000 clay tablets, four times as many as all the earlier known records in the Middle East from this time period.

The few tablets already translated include many biblical names such as Abram, Esau, Israel, Saul, David, and Michael. Ebla's greatest king was Ebrum (or Iberium), whose name is strikingly similar to Eber (Iber, Heber) the ancestor of Abraham and the Hebrews. Also, the same five city-states of Genesis 14 show up in exactly the same order. These records also indicate many other cities and villages were in the Middle East during the patriarchal period. As more records from Ebla and other sites are translated and become available to English readers, we can begin to understand much more about the time of Abraham and his history. (For example, see Howard La Fay, "Ebla, Splendor of an Unknown Empire," *National Geographic*, Dec., 1978, pp. 731-759; Giovanni Pettinato, "The Royal Archives of Tell Mardikh-Ebla," *Biblical Archeologist*, May, 1976, pp. 44-52.)

Sarah Giving Hagar as a Second Wife
(Gen. 16:2)

Numerous ancient Near Eastern records demonstrate the practice of a barren wife (usually after at least seven years without a child) giving a second wife to her husband. Even in a patriarchal society the husband did not automatically have the right to acquire a second wife without the first wife's permission. The fact that Sarah set such a noble example with this practice led to perhaps the only place in the scriptures where a law was named after a woman. We read about the laws of different kings and the law of Moses, but the law of plural marriage is called the "law of Sarah." (D&C 132:65.)

Circumcision, a Preparatory Ordinance to Baptism
(Gen. 17:10)

During the time of Abraham, the people had corrupted almost every element of baptism. They sprinkled rather than immersed those baptized. They baptized children before the age of accountability. They used blood instead of water. And they supposed that the blood of ancient Abel was the atoning sacrifice, rather than anticipating the future Christ and his atonement.

Therefore, they were given the law of circumcision and commanded to circumcise their children at eight days of age that they might remember that children were not accountable to the Lord until they were eight years old, when they were to be baptized. And they were instructed to keep all the other covenants as they had been commanded. (See JST Gen. 17:3-7, 11-12; BD "Circumcision." Compare D&C 74.)

In later Jewish history, they continued the practice of circumcision while gradually abandoning the ordinance of baptism, although Orthodox Judaism still requires a "washing" for all converts. The initiates are dressed in white and immersed completely under the water. A priest supervises with at least two male witnesses. Even so, they have largely neglected the primary ordinance of baptism while retaining the ordinance of circumcision.

Abimelech
(Gen. 20:2-18; 21:22-32; 26:1-31)

A king or kings of Gerar (in the land of the Philistines) named Abimelech associated with Abraham and Isaac over the course of about one hundred years. Two or more kings of the city may have carried the same name. In fact, the name "Abimelech" means "my father—a king," which easily could have been a title or hereditary name. Or, Abimelech may have been one king who lived a long time.

His first episode with Abraham and Sarah came at the time she carried Isaac. Abimelech desired Sarah as a wife or concubine, but the Lord spoke to him in a dream to prevent him from such action, which, if it had succeeded, would have brought Isaac's paternity into question. Shortly thereafter Abraham and Abimelech made a covenant of peace at Beersheba (21:22-32).

Much later, a king named Abimelech desired Isaac's wife, Rebekah, after they had resided in Gerar for a long time as "brother and sister." After a time, however, Abimelech recognized that Isaac and Rebekah were husband and wife, and protected them and later made a covenant with Isaac preserving the grazing and water rights for their respective flocks (26:1-31).

Hand under the Thigh
(Gen. 24:2, 9)

Placing a hand under the upper leg or thigh of a seated person was a solemn means of concluding an oath or contract, similar to "shaking hands" on an agreement in our society. Abraham requested this from his servant, and later Jacob asked for the same sign from his son Joseph. (See Gen. 47:29.) In the Abraham episode the Joseph Smith Translation changes the word "thigh" to "hand," meaning "put your hand under my hand" as a sign of the covenant.

Birthright Inheritance and Birthright Blessing
(Gen. 25:31-34)

The firstborn son had the first right to receive the birthright inheritance and the birthright blessing. The birthright inheritance dealt with physical property, such as flocks and herds. Unless the father had determined otherwise (see Gen. 48:5; 1 Chr. 5:1, 2) at the father's death, the physical property was to be divided into balanced portions equal to the number of sons, plus one. The eldest son received the double portion. (Deut. 21:17.) With the inheritance, he assumed responsibility for his mother and unmarried sisters. He also was to be a financial resource for his brothers in times of hardship. Basically he provided for the physical welfare of the family and usually served as the social-political leader of the family or clan.

The birthright blessing was spiritual. In the patriarchal order of the priesthood, it included the keys of the priesthood and the authority to preside as the religious leader of the family or clan. Rather than automatically belonging to the eldest son, it was given to the most righteous son. In fact, for all the patriarchal families with more than one son, the birthright blessing went to a younger son: Shem, Abraham, Isaac, Jacob, Joseph, and Ephraim each received the birthright blessing even though none of them was an eldest son.

One reason why some negative, almost sordid information was given in Genesis about some of the sons in these families was to demonstrate why they had lost the birthright blessings.

The prerogative for both the birthright inheritance and the birthright blessing originally rested exclusively with the father. He could give gifts (as Abraham did to Keturah's sons in Gen. 25:6), pass out the inheritance (compare the story of the prodigal son who received his early in Luke 15:11-12) and pronounce the blessing. (See Gen. 27:30-36.) Jacob received his blessing initially through deceit, but eventually acquired it in full integrity. (See Gen. 27:30-36; 28:1-4.) After the time of Moses, the inheritance automatically went to the eldest son, regardless of whether or not his mother was the first or favored wife. (See Deut. 21: 15-17.) The birthright blessing was still conditional.

Bible Dictionary references: Firstborn; Birthright; Inheritance.

Blessings of Judah
(Gen. 49:9-10)

The tribe of Judah received three special promises under the hand of Jacob:

1. Judah would be a tribe of courageous warriors.
2. The kingdom of Judah would remain intact until the coming of the Messiah. (They were intact as a social group and political entity under the Romans when Jesus was born, and they have maintained their identity and are again a political power in these last days before his second coming.)
3. The Messiah would come from this tribe riding on a donkey. (Zech. 9:9; Matt. 21:2-5.)

Blessings of Joseph
(Gen. 49:22-26)

Joseph received from Jacob many special promises that covered a number of conditions that would come upon his descendants. They included:

1. His posterity would go beyond Canaan unto the everlasting hills (in America).
2. His descendants would be subjected to war, but they would be blessed of the Lord and victorious in the end.
3. His tribe would receive the blessings of heaven (spirit paradise?) above.
4. His tribe would receive the blessings of the deep (missionary work in spirit prison?) below.
5. His descendants would have the blessings of breasts and wombs (great fertility and strength).
6. His tribe would carry on the blessings of the fathers (the birthright).

Prophecies of Joseph of Egypt Compared
(Gen. 50)

(Note: Italics indicate differences in the two versions.)

JST Genesis 50   2 Nephi 3

24. *And Joseph said unto his brethren, I die, and go unto my fathers; and I go down to my grave with joy. The God of my father Jacob be with you, to deliver you out of affliction in the days of your bondage; for the Lord hath visited me, and I have* obtained a promise of the Lord, that out of the fruit of *my* loins, the Lord God *will* raise up a righteous branch *out of my loins; and unto thee, whom my father Jacob hath named Israel, a prophet;* (not the Messiah *who is called Shilo;*) *and this prophet shall deliver my people out of Egypt in the days of thy bondage.*

25. *And it shall come to pass that they shall be scattered again; and* a branch *shall* be broken off, *and shall be carried into a far country;* nevertheless *they shall* be remembered in the covenants of the Lord, *when* the Messiah *cometh; for he shall* be made manifest unto them in the latter days, in the Spirit of power; *and shall* bring them out of darkness *into* light; out of hidden darkness, and out of captivity unto freedom.

26. A seer shall the Lord my God raise up, who shall be a choice seer unto the fruit of my loins.

27. Thus saith the Lord *God of my fathers* unto me, A choice seer will I raise up out of the fruit of thy loins, and he shall be esteemed highly among the fruit of thy loins; and unto him will I give commandment that he shall do a

5. *Wherefore, Joseph truly saw our day. And he* obtained a promise of the Lord, that out of the fruit of *his* loins the Lord God *would* raise up a righteous branch *unto the house of Israel;* not the Messiah, *but* a branch *which was to* be broken off, nevertheless, *to* be remembered in the covenants of the Lord *that* the Messiah *should* be made manifest unto them in the latter days, in the spirit of power, *unto the bringing of* them out of darkness *unto* light—*yea,* out of hidden darkness and out of captivity unto freedom.

6. *For Joseph truly testified, saying:* A seer shall the Lord my God raise up, who shall be a choice seer unto the fruit of my loins.

7. *Yea, Joseph truly said:* Thus saith the Lord unto me: A choice seer will I raise up out of the fruit of thy loins; and he shall be esteemed highly among the fruit of thy loins. And unto him will I give commandment that he shall do a

work for the fruit of thy loins,
his brethren.

28. *And he shall bring* them
to the knowledge of the covenants which I have made with
thy fathers; *and he shall do what-*
soever work I shall command him.

29. And I will make him
great in mine eyes, for he shall
do my work; and he shall be
great like unto *him* whom I
have said I would raise up unto
you, to deliver my people, O
house of Israel, *out of the land of*
Egypt; for a seer will I raise up to
deliver my people out of the land of
Egypt; and he shall be called
Moses. And by this name he shall
know that he is of thy house; for he
shall be nursed by the king's daugh-
ter, and shall be called her son.

30. *And again,* a seer will I
raise up out of the fruit of thy
loins, and unto him will I give
power to bring forth my word
unto the seed of thy loins; and
not to the bringing forth *of* my
word only, saith the Lord, but
to the convincing them of my
word, which shall have already
gone forth among them *in the*
last days;

31. Wherefore the fruit of
thy loins shall write, and the
fruit of the loins of Judah shall
write; and that which shall be
written by the fruit of thy loins,
and also that which shall be
written by the fruit of the loins
of Judah, shall grow together
unto the confounding of false
doctrines, and laying down of
contentions, and establishing
peace among the fruit of thy
loins, and bringing them to *a*
knowledge of their fathers in

work for the fruit of thy loins,
his brethren, *which shall be of*
great worth unto them, even to the
bringing of them to the knowledge of the covenants which I
have made with thy fathers.

8. *And I will give unto him a*
commandment that he shall do none
other work, save the work which I
shall command him. And I will
make him great in mine eyes;
for he shall do my work.

9. And he shall be great
like unto *Moses,* whom I have
said I would raise up unto you,
to deliver my people, O house
of Israel.

10. *And Moses will I raise up,*
to deliver thy people out of the land
of Egypt.

11. *But* a seer will I raise
up out of the fruit of thy loins;
and unto him will I give power
to bring forth my word unto
the seed of thy loins—and not
to the bringing forth my word
only, saith the Lord, but to the
convincing them of my word,
which shall have already gone
forth among them.

12. Wherefore, the fruit of
thy loins shall write; and the
fruit of the loins of Judah shall
write; and that which shall be
written by the fruit of thy loins,
and also that which shall be
written by the fruit of the loins
of Judah, shall grow together,
unto the confounding of false
doctrines and laying down of
contentions, and establishing
peace among the fruit of thy
loins, and bringing them to *the*
knowledge of their fathers in

the latter days; and also to the knowledge of my covenants, saith the Lord.

32. And out of weakness *shall he* be made strong, in that day when my work shall *go forth* among all my people, *which shall restore them, who are of the* house of Israel, *in the last days.*

33. *And* that seer will *I* bless, and they that seek to destroy him shall be confounded; for this promise *I give unto you; for I will remember you from generation to generation;* and his name shall be called *Joseph,* and it shall be after the name of his father; and he shall be like unto *you;* for the thing which the Lord shall bring forth by his hand shall bring my people unto salvation.

34. *And the Lord sware* unto *Joseph that he would* preserve *his* seed forever, *saying,* I will raise up Moses, and a rod *shall be in his hand, and he shall gather together my people, and he shall lead them as a flock, and he shall smite the waters of the Red Sea with his rod.*

35. *And he shall have* judgment, *and shall write the word of the Lord. And* he shall *not* speak *many words,* for I will write unto him my law by the finger of mine own hand. And I will make a spokesman for him, *and his name shall be called Aaron.*

the latter days, and also to the knowledge of my covenants, saith the Lord.

13. And out of weakness *he shall* be made strong, in that day when my work shall *commence* among all my people, *unto the restoring thee, O* house of Israel, *saith the Lord.*

14. *And thus prophesied Joseph, saying: Behold,* that seer will *the Lord* bless; and they that seek to destroy him shall be confounded; for this promise, *which I have obtained of the Lord, of the fruit of my loins, shall be fulfilled. Behold, I am sure of the fulfilling of this promise;*

15. And his name shall be called *after me;* and it shall be after the name of his father. And he shall be like unto *me;* for the thing, which the Lord shall bring forth by his hand, *by the power of the Lord* shall bring my people unto salvation.

16. *Yea, thus prophesied Joseph: I am sure of this thing, even as I am sure of the promise of Moses; for the Lord hath said* unto *me, I will* preserve *thy* seed forever.

17. *And the Lord hath said:* I will raise up *a* Moses; and *I will give power unto him in* a rod; *and I will give* judgment *unto him in writing. Yet I will not loose his tongue, that* he shall speak *much,* for *I will not make* him *mighty in speaking. But* I will write unto him my law, by the finger of mine own hand; and I will make a spokesman for him.

Exodus

Like the book of Genesis, the first twenty chapters of Exodus are familiar to most Latter-day Saints. However, the later portions of this "Second Book of Moses" often confuse and frustrate readers. These problems continue through the rest of the five books of Moses (also known as the Pentateuch, the Books of the Law, or the Torah). To better appreciate these five books, review them from the context of the Israelites during the time of Moses and note how these detailed, particular instructions were necessary to separate them from their Egyptian paganism and to prepare them for their settlement in the promised land (note that the Jaredites, Nephites, and Mormon pioneers also went through long periods of travel, testing, and teaching before they reached their own lands of promise). Then try to evaluate the principles or higher laws behind all the laws, commandments, and stories of this period of Israelite history. Finally, try to apply these principles and higher laws to life today and compare them to the laws of the gospel. Such a threefold approach to this material will take it from the realm of dry, historical past and place it within the struggles and challenges of contemporary life.

The book of Exodus is often divided into three segments:
1. The Hebrews in bondage (1-12).
2. Their exodus and travels to Sinai (13-19).
3. God's laws for Israel and the Tabernacle (20-40).

Bible Dictionary references:
1. In Bondage (1-12): Exodus, Book of; Moses; Burning Bush; Egypt; Pithon; Pharaoh; Leaven.
2. Exodus and Wilderness (13-19): Red Sea; Wilderness of the Exodus; Manna; Sinai.
3. Commandments and Laws (20-24): Commandments, The Ten; Shechinah; Law of Moses; Feasts; Firstfruits; Elders.
4. Tabernacle and Priests (25-40): Tabernacle; Symbolism; Altar; Shewbread; Candlestick; Incense; Ark of the Covenant; Mercy Seat; Cherubim; High Priest; Laying on of hands; Ephod; Embroidery; Breastplate; Urim and Thummim; Daily Service; Cloud.

See also Map 3.

How Could Moses Abide in God's Presence?
(Exodus 3:6)

A modern prophet, Spencer W. Kimball, has given a clear answer to this question:

> It must be obvious, then, that to endure the glory of the Father or of the glorified Christ, a mortal being must be translated or otherwise fortified.
>
> Grease on the swimmer's body or a heavy rubber skin-diver's suit may protect one from cold and wet; an asbestos suit might protect a firefighter from flames; a bullet-proof vest may save one from assassin's bullets; one's heated home may protect from winter's chilling blasts; deep shade or smoked glass can modify the withering heat and burning rays of the midday sun. There is a protective force that God brings into play when he exposes his human servants to the glories of his person and his works.
>
> Moses, a prophet of God, held the protecting holy priesthood: ". . . and the glory of God was upon Moses; therefore Moses could endure his presence." (Moses 1:2.)
>
> In heavenly glorious vision, Moses "beheld the world . . . and all the children of men. . . ." (Moses 1:8.) He was protected then, but when the protection from such transcendent glory was relaxed, Moses was left near-helpless. (FPM, p. 86.)

Joseph [Smith] had had the same general experience as Abraham and Moses and Enoch, who had seen the Lord and heard his voice. In addition, he heard the Father, bearing witness of the Son, as had Peter, James, and John on Transfiguration's mount. He had seen the person of Elohim. He had fought a desperate battle with the powers of darkness as had Moses and Abraham. And like them all, he was protected by the glory of the Lord. . . .

In light of the testimony of Joseph Smith, the ancient scriptures take on new meaning, their literal verity confirmed by the experience of modern man who, quickened and protected by the Spirit, actually saw the Father and the Son. How great a blessing to see God and commune directly with him while yet in mortality! Though few of us will have that blessing, we can, through understanding the scriptures and by humble prayer, come in impressive measure to know God. We have the promise that if we sufficiently purify our hearts we shall surely see God and know him as he is! (FPM, p. 93.)

Why Was Moses Chosen by the Lord?
(Ex. 3:11)

From the human viewpoint, the ancient Israelites probably had many reasons to reject Moses as the Lord's prophet:

1. His pagan background for forty years in the royal courts of Egypt (2:10).
2. His having killed the Egyptian overseer (2:11-15).
3. His forty-year separation from Israel (2:16-25).
4. His lack of self-confidence when receiving the call (3:6, 11, 13; 4:1, 10, 13).
5. His stubbornness (4:24-26).
6. His easy discouragement after being rejected by Pharaoh (5:20-23; 6:12, 30).
7. His old age of eighty years (7:7).

However, the Lord knew the power and potential of this great prophet, and with the Lord's support and power, Moses was able to lead Israel out of bondage.

Genealogy of Moses
(Ex. 6:16-20)

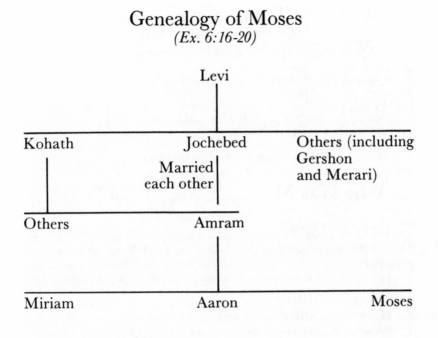

Levi

Kohath	Jochebed	Others (including Gershon and Merari)
	Married each other	
Others	Amram	
Miriam	Aaron	Moses

Preparation for the Theophany
(Ex. 19:19-25)

The Israelites spent two days cleansing themselves physically and spiritually prior to the manifestation of God to them on Mount Sinai. As a whole community, they heard the voice of the Lord as he delivered the Ten Commandments. (See Deut. 4:33; 5:4, 24.) This experience so humbled and terrified them that they requested that any future words from the Lord should come through Moses. (See Ex. 20:18-22; Deut. 5:5, 23-33.)

The Ten Commandments
(Ex. 20:1-17; Deut. 5:6-21)
President Spencer W. Kimball explained:

Through Moses the word of the Lord came down from the mountain. The commandments which the Lord gave to the children of Israel set minimum standards of conduct. These commandments, said Paul, are "our schoolmaster to bring us unto Christ, that we might be justified by faith" (Gal. 3:24).

But living by the letter of the Ten Commandments is only the beginning of perfection. Jesus taught the sanctity of the Ten Commandments, but emphasized repeatedly that there was more.

It is not enough to acknowledge the Lord as supreme and refrain from worshiping idols; we should love the Lord with all our heart, might, mind, and strength, realizing the great joy he has in the righteousness of his children.

It is not enough to refrain from profanity or blasphemy. We need to make important in our lives the name of the Lord. While we do not use the Lord's name lightly, we should not leave our friends or our neighbors or our children in any doubt as to where we stand. Let there be no doubt about our being followers of Jesus Christ.

It is not enough to refrain from moviegoing, hunting, fishing, sports, and unnecessary labor on the Sabbath. Constructive use of the Sabbath day includes studying the scriptures, attending church meetings to learn and to worship, writing letters to absent loved ones, comforting the sorrowing, visiting the sick, and, in general, doing what the Lord would have us do on this, his holy day.

If we truly honor our parents as we are commanded to do, we will seek to emulate their best characteristics and to fulfill their highest aspirations for us. Nothing we could give them materially would be more prized than our righteous living.

It is not enough to refrain from killing. We are rather under solemn obligation to respect life and to foster it. Far from taking a life, we must be generous in helping others to enjoy the necessities of life. And when this has been accomplished, we seek to improve the mind and the spirit.

We refrain from taking harmful substances into our body. Through wisdom and moderation in all things, we seek good health and a sense of physical well-being.

It is not enough to refrain from adultery. We need to make the marriage relationship sacred, to sacrifice and work to maintain the warmth and respect which we enjoyed during courtship. God intended marriage to be eternal, sealed by the power of the priesthood, to last beyond the grave. Daily acts of courtesy and kindness, conscientiously and lovingly carried out, are part of what the Lord expects.

It is for us to keep our hearts and minds pure, as well as our actions.

"Thou shalt not steal," the Lord said on Sinai (Exod. 20:15). Thus it is for us to be honest in every way. We must be generous, the very opposite of selfishness. When money is needed, we give money. But often what is needed more is love and time and caring, which money cannot buy. When that is true, even being generous with our money is not enough.

Bearing false witness and coveting the belongings of others are further evidence of selfishness. "Love thy neighbour as thyself," Jesus taught. On this and on the love of God "hang all the law and the prophets" (Matt. 22:39-40).

Kindness, helpfulness, love, concern, generosity—we could go on for the list of virtues is endless. The development of these traits is what the Lord asks of us. (*Ensign,* Nov., 1978, p. 6.)

What Is the Law of Moses?
(Ex. 21:1)

The law of Moses encompasses hundreds of laws, rules, and regulations. The Jews have identified 613 particular laws as recorded by Moses in the books of the Torah (or the Pentateuch: Genesis, Exodus, Leviticus, Numbers, and Deuteronomy). The Ten Commandments and other familiar laws are included in this body, but most of the laws are unfamiliar, and seem outdated and strange to contemporary Bible readers.

Rather than trying to identify every single law, it is helpful to recognize that there are two major types of commandments within the law of Moses—eternal and temporary.

The eternal laws are those divine commandments that have been given to most, if not all, of the gospel dispensations. Included among these eternal laws are:

1. First principles and ordinances of the gospel (faith, repentance, baptism, gift of the Holy Ghost).
2. Tithing.
3. Offerings and charity for the needy.
4. Legislation for justice, brotherhood, fairness, and so on.
5. Simple sacrifice (in similitude of the Only Begotten; our sacrament fills this purpose today).
6. The Ten Commandments.

The temporary laws were given for a particular dispensation. However, similar laws or "carnal commandments" were usually given to other dispensations to fulfill similar purposes. Sometimes these peculiar laws were to test the obedience of God's children, but they usually had symbolic, physical, and social values as well. Included among them would be the following types of laws:

1. Religious festivals and holy days (comparable to Easter, Christmas, general conference, and Thanksgiving).
2. Elaborate system of special sacrifices and offerings (comparable to the multitude of meetings, callings, and responsibilities within the Church today).
3. Particular ordinances, usually symbolic of ceremonial cleanliness (comparable to the baptism and temple work today).
4. Dietary laws (the ancient "Word of Wisdom").
5. Laws of purification or sanitation (city and government bodies usually regulate similar affairs in contemporary society).

The Tabernacle
(Ex. 26)

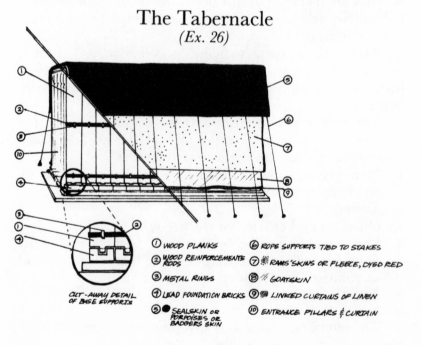

CUT-AWAY DETAIL OF BASE SUPPORTS

① WOOD PLANKS
② WOOD REINFORCEMENT RODS
③ METAL RINGS
④ LEAD FOUNDATION BRICKS
⑤ SEALSKIN OR PORPOISES OR BADGERS SKIN
⑥ ROPE SUPPORTS TIED TO STAKES
⑦ RAMS'SKINS OR FLEECE, DYED RED
⑧ GOATSKIN
⑨ LINKED CURTAINS OF LINEN
⑩ ENTRANCE PILLARS & CURTAIN

Robes of the Levitical Priesthood
(Ex. 28, 29, 39)

There were three divisions or offices in the Levitical Priesthood: Levite, priest, and high priest. Officers of these divisions wore special attire. These vestments are mentioned and sometimes described in the scriptures (see TG "Clothing," "Garment," "Robe," "Breastplate," and "Apparel") and in later rabbinical literature. The main items included:

1. Linen breeches and/or tunic, garment: white, short-sleeved, knee-length; worn by all officers. (See Lev. 6:10, 11).
2. Linen robe: white, short or no sleeves, between knee and ankle length; worn by the priests and high priest.
3. Girdle or sash: white (?), wrapped around the robe at waist; worn by the priests and high priest.
4. Mitre or bonnet, cap: white (or blue?), bell or blossom shaped; worn by the priests and high priest.
5. Robe or coat: blue, seamless collar, near ankle length, gold bells and (embroidered?) pomegranates on hem; only worn by the high priest.
6. Ephod or apron, poncho: woven of (real) gold, blue, purple, and scarlet threads, hung from both shoulders, tied with girdle of similar fabric, two engraved stones set in the shoulders from which gold chains joined to breastplate; worn only by the high priest. (See BD "Ephod.")
7. Breastplate: woven fabric like the ephod folded over to make pouch (in which the Urim and Thummim were kept), twelve engraved stones in gold casings mounted on front, joined to ephod shoulders by gold chains and to ephod girdle-sash through gold rings at bottom; worn only by the high priest. (See BD "Breastplate.")
8. Golden plate: attached with blue thread to cap, engraved with "Holiness to the Lord"; worn only by the high priest.

Robes of the High Priest
(Ex. 28-29)

Washing or Baptizing the Priests
(Ex. 29:4)

According to the great rabbinical commentator, Rashi, the Hebrew verb in this verse translated as "wash" signifies "immersion" of the whole body. (*Soncino Chumash*, p. 527.) The word *baptism* (Greek) was unknown to the Israelites. They used the word *rochatz*, which is usually translated as "wash" or "washing."

Leviticus

Leviticus is an unknown, almost "sealed" book to most Latter-day Saints. Most of the ritual laws and sacrifices in this book are not easily understood. Indeed, most of them are no longer practiced by Jews, Christians, or Moslems, although all three religions recognize the scriptural validity of this work. But rather than discarding Leviticus as a meaningless set of archaic religious laws, one should evaluate the role of these laws within ancient Israel. Then one can appreciate how: the symbolism of the sacrifices directed Israel toward Christ (1-7); the example of Aaron and his sons taught them about service (8-10); the laws of purification kept them physically and spiritually clean (11-15); the Day of Atonement forced them to annually evaluate their lives in preparation for the final day of judgment (16); the code of holiness distinguished them as a peculiar people, in the world but not of the world (17-25); and the promises and vows between the Lord and his people guaranteed them a special, eternal relationship (26).

The following introduction to Leviticus highlights some of its values:

Leviticus is essentially a rule-book—the book of laws given by God to his people through Moses at Sinai. The laws cover ritual and worship and many aspects of life—but all seen in relation to him. The book takes its name from the fact that it was the Levitical priests (Aaron and his sons and descendants, helped in the practical work of the tabernacle

by the rest of the Levites) who administered the laws. But the book is
not for the priests alone. God intended all his people to know and keep
his law. Again and again Moses is told to 'speak to the people of Israel'.

To many modern readers it may seem a strange book, perhaps even
a repulsive one with all its blood-sacrifices. Some see it as reflecting
only an odd set of ancient taboos. Yet take it away and whole areas of
Scripture become inexplicable. Without the message of Leviticus the
key event of all time, the [Atonement and] death of Jesus Christ, is an
enigma. The ritual and the rules were never simply an end in themselves. As the sacrifices were performed day after day, year after year, as
the Day of Atonement came and went, Israel was constantly reminded
of the sin which cut them off from God's presence. They had broken
covenant with God by disobeying his laws and were under sentence of
death. But God in his mercy showed them that he would accept a
substitute—the death of an animal, perfect and blameless, instead of
the offender. God was holy—a moral holiness unknown in the gods of
the nations around. He demanded holiness in his people. The laws on
ritual purity hammered this home in practical everyday experience.

Yet the book has value apart from its vital role in God's message of
salvation. The laws in Leviticus show God working in harmony with
his own natural laws for the good of his people. Although Israel had to
obey the laws in blind trust (when they chose to do so at all), we can see
how those laws were actually working for the nation's health and
well-being. Because we know more today about the sources of infection
and pollution, about quarantine and isolation, hygiene and preventive
medicine, we can watch Israel's obedience actually fulfilling God's
promise to take away their sickness (Exodus 23:25). And this not by
magic, but by the natural working of principles we now, at least in part,
can understand. (David and Pat Alexander, eds., *Eerdman's Handbook to
the Bible* [Grand Rapids: William B. Eerdmans Publishing Co., 1973],
p. 172.)

Bible Dictionary references:
1. Sacrifices (1-7): Leviticus; Sacrifices; Meat; Meat Offering; Blood.
2. Priests (8-10): Aaron; Aaronic Priesthood; Levites;
   Eleazar; Baptism.
3. Purification (11-15): Clean and Unclean; Kosher;
   Purification; Leper; Leprosy.
4. Day of Atonement (16): Fasts; Scapegoat.
5. Holiness Code (17-26): Holiness; Blood (review again);
   Agriculture; Sabbatical Year; Jubilee, Year of; Redemption.

The Offerings of the Israelites
(Lev. 5-7)

1. The *burnt offering* consisted of the slaying and burning of a bullock, a ram, or a turtledove or pigeon. It produced "a sweet savour unto the Lord"; in other words, it was pleasing to him.

It was also sometimes called the whole burnt offering because the whole animal was consumed upon the altar. The altar was "the table of the Lord" (Mal. 1:7, 12; Ps. 23:5) and whatever was put upon it was the "food of God" (Lev. 21:6, 8, 17, 21).

Procedure: (1) The person brought an unblemished male animal to the gate and dedicated it as an offering by laying his hands upon the animal's head. (2) He then slew the animal. (3) The priests collected the blood and sprinkled it around the altar. (4) The person skinned the animal (the priest kept the skin [Lev. 7:8]), and cut it into pieces. (5) The priests offered the pieces upon the altar after washing the inwards and legs with water.

This offering was a continuation of the sacrifice inaugurated in the days of Adam (Moses 5:4-8), and practiced by various individuals on down to the time of Jacob. It represented the spotless sacrifice of the Savior. Under the law of Moses there was a burnt offering of lamb each morning and each night on behalf of all Israel. (Ex. 29:38-42.) The morning sacrifice was to burn all day, and the evening sacrifice was to burn all night. (Lev. 6:9.) The priests were to see that the fire of the altar was kept burning perpetually. (Lev. 6:13.)

2. The *meal offering* is called a meat offering or a food offering in some Bible editions. Today "meat" (the term used in the King James Version) implies flesh, whereas this offering was of the fruits of the field. This offering produced "a sweet savour unto the Lord."

This offering took several forms. Usually it was in the form of fine flour that would be given raw or as baked cakes. The ingredients of the offering included flour, oil, frankincense, and salt. Honey and leaven were not to be used.

Only a "memorial" or portion of this offering was burnt upon the altar. The main part of it was to be eaten by the priests and their families.

3. The *peace offering* involved the slaying of an umblemished animal, either male or female. A portion of the animal was burnt upon the altar producing a "sweet savour offering."

This was an offering shared by the altar of God, the priest, and the family of the person making the offering. It was a feast of conciliation, a feast of communion, a feast of thanksgiving. The sacrificial victim could be chosen from among the cattle, the sheep, or the goats. As the animal was brought to the door of the tabernacle, the owner laid his hands upon its head and offered a prayer of thanksgiving. Therefore this offering is sometimes called a thank offering. After the animal was killed at the altar, the kidneys and internal fat were burned on the altar. The breast and the ·right thigh were given to the priest after they had been waved in the direction of the tabernacle, thereby signifying that it had been given to God and was now conferred upon his servants. (Lev. 7:28-34.) The rest of the meat was eaten by the offerer and his family at a so-called "sacrificial" meal, or meal of "thanksgiving." (Lev. 7:15-16.)

4. The *sin offering* consisted of slaying a young, un-blemished bullock and then burning part of it upon the altar and the rest of it upon a fire "without the camp." This did not produce a sweet savour unto the Lord.

This offering was made for sins committed in ignorance but subsequently discovered. It was for offenses that could not be undone or repaired. If the offense could be repaired, a trespass offering was made. The ritual for a sin offering varied according to the rank of the offender. One distinc-tion of the sin offering from the regular burnt offering was the disposition of the blood. The priest smeared the blood of the victim on the horns of the altar of incense inside the tabernacle and then poured out the rest at the base of the brazen altar of sacrifice outside. On the annual Day of Atonement the distinctive aspect of the sin offering was the fact that the priest took some of the blood into the holy of holies and sprinkled it before the mercy seat. (Lev. 16:14.)

A portion of the animal (the internal fat and the kidneys) was burned upon the altar and the rest of the animal was taken outside the camp to be burned in the area where the ashes of the altar were poured out.

5. The *trespass offering* was also called the guilt offering. Like the sin offering, it was not a sweet savour offering.

This offering was appropriate in those cases where a person discovered that he had sinned or trespassed against the Lord or his neighbor, and was able to remedy or repair the damage. (Lev. 5:16; 6:4-5.) The scripture suggests two types of offenses for which the trespass offering would be appropriate. One was where a person found that he had held back or consumed something that belonged to the Lord such as tithes or firstborn of flocks. (Lev. 5:15.) The penalty was not only to restore to the sanctuary of the Lord that which had been withheld, but to add one-fifth thereto as a penalty. (Lev. 5:16.) A second kind of offense was where something had been withheld or disallowed to a neighbor by deceit. (Lev. 6:2-3.) Here again he had to restore that which had been lost by his neighbor plus one-fifth of its value for a penalty.

6. The *drink offering* was often used to express thanksgiving to the Lord. It consisted of the fourth part of a hin of wine (Lev. 23:13), or about three pints. This offering was simply a libation poured out before the Lord. This offering occurred every morning and every night along with the burnt offering and the meat (meal) offering. (Ex. 29:39-40.)

7. The *wave offering*, sometimes called the heave offering, was performed in connection with a peace offering (Lev. 8:29), the firstfruits of the harvest (Lev. 23:11-12), and of the two loaves at the Feast of Weeks (Lev. 23:20). It was also used in connection with the cleansing of a leper. (Lev. 14:12, 24.) The "waving" or "heaving" consisted of taking the breast and the right shoulder of a sacrificial animal or the firstfruits of the harvest and moving them

horizontally in the direction of the sanctuary. It was to signify that these choice parts of the sacrifice were first presented to God and then returned to the officiating priests for their use.

Responsibilities of the Levitical Priesthood
(Lev. 9:8-22)

The high priest (Aaron and his male descendants), priests (all male descendants of Moses and Aaron), and Levites (other male descendants of Levi) had many duties in ancient Israel. Some responsibilities were restricted to particular offices, while most of them were done jointly. Among them were:

1. Use Urim and Thummim (Ex. 28:30; Num. 27:21); high priest only.
2. Administer worship in the tabernacle (or later in the temple: Lev. 24:5-9; Ex. 30:7-10, 22-38); high priest and priests.
3. Serve as religious judges in Israel (Lev. 13, 14; Num. 35:6-32); high priest and priests.
4. Care for sacred articles of tabernacle or temple (Num. 4:5-20); high priest and priests.
5. Supervise circumcisions, washings, and baptisms (Ex. 40:12; Josh. 5:8; D&C 84:26-27); priests.
6. Assist in sacrifices (Lev. 6:12, 9:13, Ex. 29:38-44); high priest (Day of Atonement), priests, and Levites.
7. Teach Israel the laws and covenants (Lev. 10:11; Deut. 33:10); all offices.
8. Collect and distribute tithes and offerings (Lev. 9:16-22); all offices.
9. Move tabernacle and maintain tabernacle and fences (later temple and courtyards: Num. 3:5-13, 23-37; 4); all offices.
10. Blow the silver trumpets to announce religious festivals and holy days or to call men to war (Num. 10:1-8); Levites.
11. Work in all types of service at the tabernacle or temple (1 Chr. 6:48); Levites.

Although the contemporary holders of the Aaronic Priesthood do not have all these responsibilities, they continue in some of them, and much of their work and service compares to the responsibilities of the ancient Levites. One can make many comparisons between these two groups of priesthood holders.

Justice under the Law of Moses
(Lev. 19:15)

The Law of Moses is usually considered a harsh system of justice, but in many ways it was more fair and helpful to individuals and society than our current system of justice. Justice under the Law of Moses had three main criteria: (1) the rights of the victim were of greatest priority, (2) the burden of responsibility rested upon the offender, and (3) the offender was helped toward repentance.

1. *Rights of the victim.* When any injustice was perpetuated upon a person, the first priority was to correct the injustice as fully as possible. The major means was to require an adequate restitution by the guilty party. It was really a system of reparation, not a law of automatic retaliation, that guided ancient Israel. The guilt, accountability, and restitution of the offender would ideally be worked out between the two parties involved in the offense. Usually, however, witnesses would come before a judge, and he would decide whether or not the person was guilty and how he could amend the situation. Thereafter, the responsibility rested upon the guilty party to best correct the problem.

2. *Burden of the offender.* The guilty person had certain rights and options. Israelite society included a system of appeals (judges of tens, fifties, hundreds, and thousands, and Moses). Later in the period of judges, both parties would need to agree upon the judge who would hear their case and they would agree to accept his judgment.

However, even after a person was found guilty of, for example, assault, and the judge ordered that he provide a strong manservant to work six months for the victim while the victim's broken arm healed, the guilty person still had at least three options: (1) he could accept the arbitrated decision of the judge, (2) he could opt for an eye for an eye (in this case a broken arm for a broken arm) if he felt the sentence was too harsh or unattainable, or (3) he could forfeit all rights as a member of Israelite society and flee the country to avoid punishment. However, this last choice would only be made in desperation or foolishness, because he would hardly be accepted in any other country on any more than the lowest level of their social order. And if he ever returned to Israel, any relative of the victim could automatically execute an eye-for-an-eye punishment.

None of these three options are pleasant, but the responsibility for the problem was upon the guilty party, and in order to satisfy justice, he had to make some choice.

Let us compare how ancient Israelite law and our system of justice would handle the same case. Suppose that two men got into an argument and started fighting. The one who started the fight knocked the other person to the ground. His head hit a rock and he is killed. The first man had not wanted to kill the other man, so he was not found guilty of murder, but of manslaughter.

In our society he would be sent to jail for a number of years, which would cost taxpayers thousands of dollars a year. In the meantime, his family and the family of the victim would both probably go on welfare, with additional burdens placed upon society. Even though the community did not commit the act, they assume the burden of the guilty person, his family, and the victim's family.

Under Israelite law, the guilty person would assume the responsibility for the victim's family while still providing for the welfare of his own family. If he refused, it would be a life for a life, so he would almost always accept the extra burden of caring for the victim's family rather than be executed or leave the country.

Direct or complete restitution was impossible in this case, since the father could not be replaced in the victim's family, but they should have some satisfaction in realizing that the guilty person was taking care of them. Compare our society, where the victim's family is left on its own and usually has only the temporary satisfaction of seeing the guilty person go to jail for a few years before he is set free, and yet they are still struggling to provide for themselves.

3. *Offender on the path of repentance.* The two most difficult steps of repentance are recognition and restitution. Both these steps are built into the Mosaic system of justice. How far the guilty person would follow through on the other steps (remorse, seeking forgiveness, etc.) would be left up to him, but he was at least pointed in the right direction. In our society, most criminals' only remorse is that they got caught, and our prisons are often "institutions of higher crime" where prisoners learn even more wickedness rather than being rehabilitated.

In summary, the Mosaic law was concerned with helping the victim. Only if a guilty party could not be found to compensate the victim would society assume the burden of caring for the victim and his family.

Society's burden was to teach and administer the system of justice, while the offender had the responsibility for reparation to the victim. The system also helped the guilty person recognize his errors and repent as he made restitution. The guilty party also had his rights, but his options were restricted to either righting the wrong or leaving the society if he could not be a positive part of it.

If the system was fairly applied, the whole society benefited, and those who erred were encouraged toward repentance and full participation in society. In many ways it was a better system of justice than our own today.

Numbers

This work records some major events at the beginning and end of the Israelite wanderings in the wilderness. In Hebrew it is called the "in the wilderness" book. It picks up the Exodus historical narrative of Israel after their eleven-month sojourn at Sinai. After explaining why Israel was not ready to enter the promised land of Canaan at that time, it skips to the end of their thirty-eight years of wandering and highlights their travels around Edom and Moab. Historical events, religious laws, biographical sketches, and other items are loosely combined into a rough chronological order. The book could be divided into three time segments:

I.   Near Mount Sinai (1-10:10)—two months.
   A. First census (1-4).
   B. Miscellaneous laws (5).
   C. Nazarite vows (6).
   D. Princely offerings (7).
   E. Miscellaneous laws (8, 9).
   F. Second Passover, fiery cloud, leaving Sinai (10).

II. Through the wilderness to Moab (11-22)—thirty-eight years.
   A. From Sinai to Paran (11-12).
      1. Murmurings (11).
      2. Miriam and Aaron complain (12).

  B. Sojourn in Paran (13-19).
      1. The spies (13-14).
      2. Miscellaneous laws (15).
      3. Rebellion of Korah and others (16-17).
      4. Service of Priests and Levites (18).
      5. Law of purification (19).
  C. From Kadesh to Moab (20-21).
      1. Traveling and deaths of Miriam and Aaron (20).
      2. Serpents near Edom and enemy conflicts in the Transjordan (21).

III. In the plains north of Moab (22-36)—five months.
  A. Balaam (22-24).
  B. Miscellaneous laws and events (25-32).
      1. Adultery and idolatry (25).
      2. Second census (26).
      3. Women's inheritance rights (27:1-11).
      4. Joshua to succeed Moses (27:12-23).
      5. Laws of public worship (28-29).
      6. Women's vows (30).
      7. War against Midian (31).
      8. Transjordan inheritances (32).
  C. Review of travels and preview of settlement (33-36).
      1. Israelite route from Egypt to Canaan (33:1-49).
      2. Israel's duty in Canaan (33:50-56).
      3. Tribal inheritances in Canaan (34).
      4. Levitical and refuge cities (35).
      5. Marriage of heiresses (36).

As many religious laws and miracles of the Lord are recorded in this book, it illustrates the divine power given to Moses as he continued to lead Israel. Although confronted by many difficulties, Moses was able to retain and magnify his leadership role. His work completed, he gathered Israel to receive his last counsel and prepare them to enter into a covenant agreement with their Lord.

Bible Dictionary references: Numbers; Priests; Kohath;

Nazarite; Hem of garment; Lots, Casting of; New Moon; Sabbath; Stranger; Usury; Eldad and Medad; Edom; Fiery Serpents; Serpent, Brazen; Gad; Reuben; Manasseh; Balaam.

The Numbers of Men
(Num. 1-3)

The first chapters in the book of Numbers record the results of three major censuses. The first was a census of all men aged twenty and older who could bear arms. The total was 603,550. (Num. 1:46.) The second census consisted of all Levite males one month and older. The total was 22,300. (Num. 3:22, 28, 34.) The last census was of all first-born males one month and older. The total was 22,273. (Num. 3:43.)

There is an obvious problem in matching the figures of the first and third censuses. If, according to the third census, there were 22,273 firstborn males one month and older (some of whom were fathers and grandfathers), one could assume there would be an approximately equal number of firstborn females one month and older. With forty-five to fifty thousand firstborn children aged one month and older, Israel at most would have had fifty thousand families (but in reality the number of families would be much less because many firstborn children would be the heads of their own families so that they and their first child would both be in the total figure). Yet even with around fifty thousand families, these families would have had to provide over six hundred thousand warriors aged twenty and older (according to the first census). That would mean *each* family would have had to provide between twelve and fifteen males over twenty years old who could bear arms. Assuming an equal number of daughters, each family would have had to have from twenty-five to thirty children *over the age of twenty* to match the two sets of figures. Obviously, the figures of one census or the other are incorrect or misinterpreted.

Many scholars support the figures of the second and third censuses, which would indicate an Israelite community of from twenty thousand to fifty thousand families for a total of one hundred thousand to two hundred fifty thousand Israelites. They argue that the figures of the first census are misinterpreted.

Chapter one lists how each tribe recorded the number of males (over age twenty) and all that could go to war. Then in the original Hebrew text, two sets of figures are listed for each tribe. For example, Numbers 1:21 says the tribe of Reuben had a total of forty-five *eleph* and five *meot*, which is usually interpreted forty-five thousand and five hundred. The second term *meot* is the plural of *meah* which appears 588 times in the Old Testament and is always translated as "hundred." However, the first term *eleph*, which frequently means *thousand*, has also been translated as "family" (Judg. 6:15), "duke" or "chief" (Gen. 36:15-36; Ex. 15:15; 1 Chr. 1:51-54), "captain" (Jer. 13:21), "chief friend" (Prov. 16:28), "friend" or "leader" (Prov. 17:9), "governor" or "clan" (Zech. 9:7; 12:5, 6), and "guide" (Ps. 55:13; Prov. 2:17; Jer. 3:4; Micah 7:5). Thus, the tribe of Reuben may have had forty-five chieftains (captains, leaders, guides, professional warriors, etc.) *or* forty-five families (companies, groups, units, squads, sets, etc.) of warriors and five hundred (of men aged twenty and older who were healthy and able to fight). The figures in Numbers 1 for all the tribes are:

Tribe	Eleph	Men
Reuben	46	500
Simeon	59	300
Gad	45	650
Judah	74	600
Issachar	54	400
Zebulun	57	400
Ephraim	40	500
Manasseh	32	200
Benjamin	35	400
Dan	62	700
Asher	41	500
Naphtali	53	400
Total	598	5,550

There are three ways these figures could be interpreted.
1. 598 "thousands" and 5550 men=603,550 warriors.
2. 598 "chieftains" and 5550 men=6,148 warriors.
3. 598 "families" and 5550 men=10,000–600,000 warriors, depending upon the size of the individual family units.

Given the facts of the third census, either option 2 or 3 would seem logical. At the time of the exodus, it is estimated that Canaan had between two and three million inhabitants. According to the biblical record, Israel was much smaller in numbers than the Canaanites (Deut. 7:7, 17, 22), and the Israelites were not able to overpower the Canaanites by sheer numbers (Ex. 23:29; Judges 1:19, 27-35).

Although outnumbered by the Canaanites, the Israelites in the wilderness were still a very large community of at least one hundred thousand and probably closer to two hundred thousand people. Imagine moving the entire population of Salt Lake City for forty years through the deserts of Nevada. Not only would the leadership of the prophet be severely tested, but a daily miracle of manna and occasionally miracles of water, quail, and so on would be required to sustain the multitude. The group of Israelites moving through Sinai required the help of God in order to survive, yet they were not large enough to invade and overpower Canaan. A figure of twenty-two thousand first-born sons and a total population of about two hundred thousand Israelites seems likely.

The Camp of Israel in the Wilderness
(Num. 4)

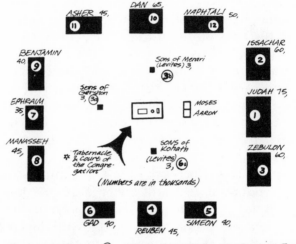

(Numbers are in thousands)

CIRCLED NUMBERS i.e. ③ = ORDER OF THIS TRIBE OR GROUP IN THE MARCH BETWEEN CAMPS

✿ SEE DETAIL BELOW

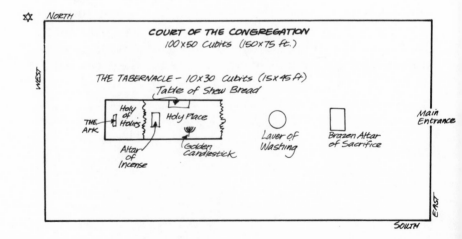

Nazarites
(Num. 6:1-21)

The term *Nazarite* comes from a Hebrew word whose root meaning is "to separate, cut off, or keep oneself from." There were two main ways that a Nazarite would "separate" himself.

First, a Nazarite would "separate from" certain products or actions. Specifically, he was not to eat any fruit of the vine (grapes, raisins, grape juice, wine, etc.). He was not to cut his hair while under the vow. And he was not to touch a dead person (even a member of his own family).

Secondly, the Nazarite would "separate toward" certain vows or obligations of his own choice. These could include personal goals, community service, religious duties, or whatever he desired. The vows were to be voluntary and from the heart.

The vow of a Nazarite lasted anywhere from a month to a lifetime. Either men or women could enter the vow (for example, Samson and his mother). Parents could even raise their child as a Nazarite and as the child matured he could decide if he wanted to honor his parents' desire and continue the vow on his own.

Noted examples of Nazarites are Samson (Judg. 13:5), Samuel (1 Sam. 1:11), and John the Baptist (Luke 1:15). The particular restrictions that separated the Nazarite from society and the vows that separated him toward personal fulfillment and social service are seen in the Church today in the missionary program. Although a Nazarite (or a missionary) seems to be sacrificing much while under their vows, they usually gain the most from such commitment and service. Both programs prepare disciplined, committed individuals who can better serve the Lord. (See BD "Nazarite.")

Moses' Transjordan Campaign
(Num. 21)

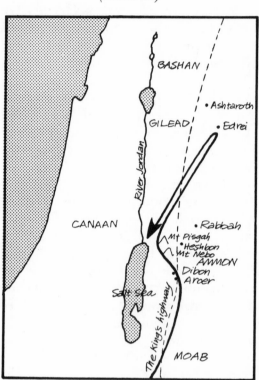

Balaam, a Prophet Who Leads Moab
and Israel into Wickedness
(Num. 22-24)

Balaam was a prophet often inspired by the Lord. The leader of the Moabites repeatedly sought out Balaam and requested him to curse Israel, but Balaam ignored the bribes and threats and only blessed Israel and prophesied of the Messiah.

Later, under circumstances not recorded, Balaam became involved again with the Moabites. He would not curse Israel for Moab's sake, but he did inform the Moabites that the Israelites would lose the grace and strength of the Lord only as they sinned. Thereafter the Moabites and Midianites enticed many Israelites into idolatry and adultery until a plague struck Israel, taking twenty-four thousand casualties. Finally Israel repented and fought against and prevailed over the Midianites. One casualty of the war was Balaam, who was killed by the Israelites. (Num. 31:16, 8; 25:1-9, 16-18; 31:1-20.)

Elder Bruce R. McConkie summarized the story of Balaam as follows:

> What a story this is! Here is a prophet of God who is firmly committed to declare only what the Lord of heaven directs. There does not seem to be the slightest doubt in his mind about the course he should pursue. He represents the Lord, and neither a house full of gold and silver nor high honors offered by the king can sway him from his determined course, which has been charted for him by that God whom he serves.
>
> But greed for wealth and lust for honor beckon him. How marvelous it would be to be rich and powerful—as well as having the prophetic powers that already are his.
>
> Perhaps the Lord would let him compromise his standards and have some worldly prosperity and power as well as a testimony of the gospel. Of course he knew the gospel was true, as it were, but why should he be denied the things his political file leader could confer?
>
> I wonder how often some of us get our direction from the Church and then, Balaam-like, plead for some worldly rewards and finally receive an answer which says, in effect, if you are determined to be a millionaire or to gain this or that worldly honor, go ahead, with the understanding that you will continue to serve the Lord. Then we wonder why things don't work out for us as well as they would have done if we had put first in our lives the things of God's kingdom?
>
> What are the rewards of unrighteousness? Do they not include seeking for worldly things when these run counter to the interests of the Church?
>
> And don't we all know people who, though they were once firm and steadfast in testimony, are now opposing the Lord's purposes and interests on earth because money and power have twisted their judgment of what should or should not be.
>
> Balaam, the prophet, inspired and mighty as he once was, lost his soul in the end because he set his heart on the things of this world rather than the riches of eternity. (Bruce R. McConkie, "The Story of a Prophet's Madness," *New Era*, Apr. 1972, p. 7.)

Importance of Vows
(Num. 30:2)

Vows made in the name of the Lord were especially sacred. If even a simple vow was made in God's name and then broken, the person could be stoned to death. Breaking the vow itself was not as serious as the taking of the Lord's name in vain.

In this dispensation we still make sacred covenants through baptism, receiving the priesthood, and in the temple ordinances. These and other public or private vows should be seriously renewed each week as we partake of the sacrament.

Deuteronomy

As the name Deuteronomy (repetition or "second-saying" of the law) may suggest, this book at first appears to be a simple restatement of the major laws and teachings of Moses. However, they are structured together in a format found in other Near Eastern records. The form of this book is very similar to the vassal treaties made between great kings and the rulers of smaller, subject states. The classical format contained the following parts:

1. Preamble ("These are the words . . .").
2. Historical prologue ("King _____ who has conquered _____").
3. General stipulations (outlining the present and future relationship between the king and his vassal, including the reasons for the specific agreements following).
4. Specific stipulations (detailed, particular contracts).
5. Divine witnesses (various deities were called upon to witness the treaty).
6. Blessings and curses (relating to the maintenance or breach of the covenant).
7. Preservation and renewal of the contract (where written, how to be maintained).

The component parts of such a treaty or covenant are seen in Deuteronomy:

1. Preamble (1:15: "These are the words of Moses . . .").
2. Historical prologue (1:6–4:49: Moses' review of the last forty years).

3. General stipulations (5-11: covenant relationship between God and Israel is outlined).
4. Specific stipulations (12-26: particular laws and obligations are reviewed).
5. Witnesses (27:1: Moses and seventy elders; 27:2-8: written record on stones; 30:19: heaven and earth; 31:19: a song; 31:26: written record and Levites; 32:1-43: Moses).
6. Curses and blessings (27-33: both for immediate generation and future dispensations).
7. Preservation and renewal of contract (27:2-8; 31:9-13, 24-27: recording and requiring future reading of the covenant).

Some scholars believe Moses or later Israelite religious leaders borrowed the vassal treaty format used between secular rulers and adapted it to the religious covenant between God and Israel. More correctly, both Moses and secular kings have followed an ancient covenant arrangement between God and man. Since the days of Adam, the people have entered into covenants with the Lord. These continue in the Church today. It is especially interesting to consider the temple ordinances from the standpoint of this classical format.

Thus, the book of Deuteronomy is more than Moses' review of his earlier teachings. It goes beyond a "last lecture" and becomes a capstone for the covenant relationship between the Lord and Israel. This covenant formula in Deuteronomy was not only for the generation of Israelites listening to Moses but it should also be accepted by each following generation:

Using the form of an address, Moses is portrayed as explaining the divine will to a new generation which had not itself experienced the formative events of its religious history. Deuteronomy, therefore, serves as a commentary on how future generations are to approach the law and it functions as a guide in establishing its canonical role. The book instructs future Israel on the manner in which past tradition is properly made alive in fresh commitment to the God of the covenant.

First, Deuteronomy emphasizes that God's covenant is not tied to past history, but is still offered to all the people. The continuity of the covenant relationship is in no way weakened by the passing of time, but in the act of commitment Israel of every age partakes of the self-same event of Sinai.

Secondly, the promise of God to his people still lies in the future. Israel's existence is characterized by an election, but this only can anticipate in faith the possession of her heritage.

Thirdly, Deuteronomy teaches that the law demands a response of commitment. The writer of the book strives to inculcate the law into the will of his people. The purpose of God remains a dynamic imperative which evokes an active choice in order to share in the living tradition of God's people.

Finally, the ability to summarize the law in terms of loving God with heart, soul and mind is a major check against all forms of legalism. The Mosiac law testifies to the living will of God whose eternal purpose for the life of his people offers the only grounds for hope and salvation. (Brevard S. Childs, *Introduction to the Old Testament as Scripture* [Philadelphia: Fortress Press, 1979], p. 224.)

Deuteronomy is the capstone of the five books of Moses. It epitomizes the Law (or Torah) of God as he teaches Israel about their covenant relationship. It is no wonder then that this book became the foundation for the later prophetic writings. Bible readers cannot fully understand Isaiah, Jeremiah, Alma, Paul, or the other prophets and apostles without appreciating how often they built upon the principles, concepts, symbolisms, and terminology of Deuteronomy as they taught and often quoted from this work. Latter-day Saints can read it and then better appreciate their role as covenant Israelites. They can study it and then evaluate their own commitments to the Lord. It can inspire readers today to improve their covenant relationship with the Lord.

Bible Dictionary references: Deuteronomy; Covenant; Frontlets; Inheritance; Peculiar; Pentateuch; Phylacteries; Punishments; Retaliation; Revenge; Torah. (Also note the quotations from Deuteronomy in the New Testament, which are listed on page 656 of the Bible Dictionary.)

Joshua

Joshua was the able successor to Moses. The book named after him was not necessarily written by him, but it was about him and his role in the conquest and settlement of Canaan. Some of his sayings and records are in the book, indicating either a writing close to Joshua's time or the availability of written records from that time period.

The book is well structured and is easily divided into two equal segments of twelve chapters as illustrated in the following outline:

I. The conquest of western Canaan (1-12).
    A. Preparations to cross the Jordan River (1).
    B. In the Jordan Valley (2-6).
        1. The spies in Jericho (2).
        2. Crossing the Jordan (3, 4).
        3. At Gilgal (5).
        4. Fall of Jericho (6).
    C. In the highlands (7-11).
        1. Campaign against Ai (7, 8).
        2. Gilseonites' deception and treaty (9).
        3. Southern campaign (10).
        4. Northern campaign (11).
    D. Review of the Conquest (12).

II. Settlement in Canaan (13-24).
    A. Tribal inheritances.

1. Inheritance of Transjordan tribes (13).
2. Inheritance of tribes west of Jordan (14-21).
   a. Process of selecting tribal areas (14).
   b. Judah's inheritance (15).
   c. Inheritance of Joseph, Ephraim, and part of Manasseh (16, 17).
   d. Rest of tribal inheritance, except Levites (18, 19).
   e. Cities of refuge and of Levites (20, 21).
B. Instructions from Joshua (22-24).
   1. Relationship with Transjordan tribes (22).
   2. Sermons to assembled tribes west of the Jordan (23, 24).
      a. Discourse to Israel (23).
      b. Reminder of their covenants (24).

This book is far from complete in the details of the conquest and provides only limited insights into the personality of Joshua, but it does illustrate how ably he led Israel after Moses. It also testifies how he and his generation followed the Lord. More importantly, this book shows the heart and hand of the Lord in settling his chosen children in a promised land.

Bible Dictionary references: Joshua; Joshua, Book of; Amorites; Ebal; Ephraim; Gerizim; Hill Country.

Why Did Joshua's Spies Go to Rahab the Harlot?
(Josh. 2)

Rahab may not have been a harlot. The Hebrew word used for *harlot* is *zonah*, which is from the same root as *mazon* meaning "food." A more correct translation might be to call her a "woman of *zonah* or 'food'," that is, a "woman innkeeper." Ancient inns often did provide harlots. However, just because a woman operated a tavern or inn did not necessarily mean she was a prostitute. (See Adam Clarke, *Clarke's Bible Commentary* [New York: Abingdon Press, n.d.] 2:11.)

Joshua's spies would have gone to Rahab's place for

lodging and in order to mingle with other travelers while gathering information on the city and the morale of its inhabitants. She was impressed with them and their religion, and thereafter lived a righteous life. New Testament writers later praised her faith and good works. (See Heb. 11:31; James 2:25.)

Some Christians even identify the Rahab of Christ's ancestry with this same woman (see Matt. 1:5), and Jewish rabbinical tradition has her as the ancestress of eight prophets and priests, including Jeremiah. (*Megillah* 14b.)

What Caused the Walls of Jericho to Fall?
(Josh. 6:20)

From limited archaeological excavations of Jericho, it appears that its walls were not as large or as strong when the Israelites attacked as in other times of its history. The small fortified mound of about seven acres was surrounded by two parallel walls, fifteen feet apart, each thirty feet high and six feet thick. These walls were made of sun-dried brick without binding straw and with dried mud filling gaps in the construction. The wall foundations were the remnants of earlier partially destroyed walls. However, in spite of these deficiencies, the walls provided an imposing barrier to the ill-equipped Israelites, who had no battering rams, catapults, or other machinery.

Two possible answers explain how the walls fell under the hand of the Lord on the seventh day as the Israelites completed their seventh march around the mound. First, their own marching and the vibrations or resonance it created would have weakened the walls, much like the pitch and resonance of a soprano's voice can shatter a goblet. This phenomenon still exists, and modern soldiers in large numbers will cross bridges and other unstable structures in "broken cadence," that is, by not marching in step or in unison with each other.

Second, Jericho sits on one of the most active earthquake fault lines in the world. The Jordan fault stretches from Mount Hermon in the north to Ethiopia in eastern

Africa. Archaeology and history both record other occasions when earthquakes have destroyed Jericho's walls.

The "miracle of Jericho" (as with all God's miracles) was through natural means. Whatever caused the walls to fall, the Israelites acted in faith as they marched around the city, and they recognized God's hand in this event.

Joshua's Central Campaign
(Josh. 6-9)

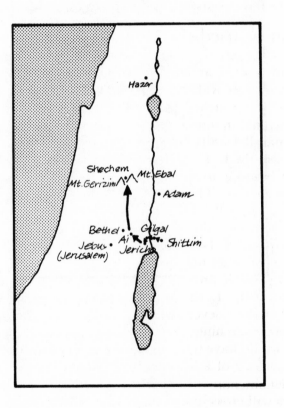

Joshua's Southern Campaign
(Josh. 10)

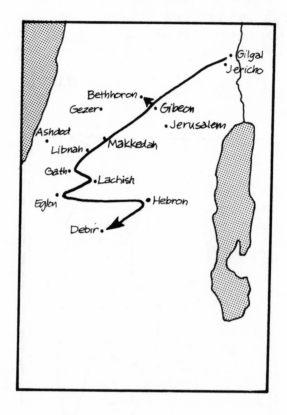

Joshua's Northern Campaign
(Josh. 11)

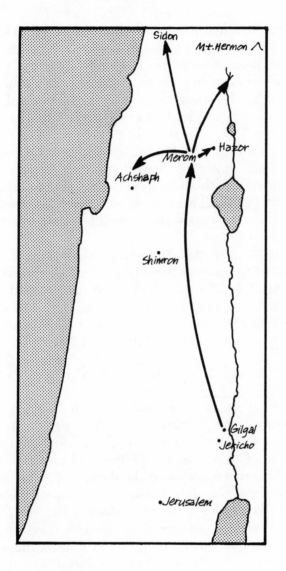

The Conquest of Canaan by Joshua and the Israelites

(Josh. 11:12-23; 13:1-7; Judg. 1)

At first reading, it appears that the Israelites easily and completely conquered Canaan under Joshua's leadership. However, more careful reading indicates that important cities and sections of Canaan, especially in the west, were not immediately brought under Israelite control. The Israelites did not conquer Canaan—they settled in the area.

Refer to Map 5 in the Bible and note how the rolling hills and plains of the Philistines and Sharon, along with the strategic valley of Jezreel and its fortress cities of Megiddo and Beth-shan, remained unconquered. These areas were (and still are) the most fertile lands in the whole country. Not to control them meant a loss of tremendous food resources.

It was the responsibility of the generations of Israelites after Joshua to conquer these lands, but they failed to do so. (See Judg. 2:20-23.) The Lord then preserved these areas and their Canaanite inhabitants from Israelite dominion for over two centuries, until they were finally subdued by David and Solomon. (See Maps 7 and 8.)

The Six Cities of Refuge

(Josh. 20)

These six cities were equidistant from each other on both sides of the Jordan River. Any person accused of murder or who had accidently killed someone else could flee to one of these Levitical cities and await a fair judgment. This process removed the danger of a vendetta from the kinsman of the slain person and allowed the elders of that city to render a more unbiased decision, like the "change of venue" process of our own legal system.

If the fugitive was found guilty of murder, he was to be delivered to the next of kin for execution. If found innocent of murder, but guilty of unpremeditated or unintentional killing, he was to remain in the city of refuge trying to maintain himself and to support his family. If he left the city, he could be slain by the kinsmen of his victim. Thus he would usually stay in the city of refuge under difficult economic and social circumstances, like a prison term, until the death of the high priest. The death of the high priest was a type of statute of limitations, and thereafter the offender could return to his home without danger of reprisal. Of course, if the fugitive was found innocent of any killing, he could immediately return home and resume his social position.

The Lord's establishment of these cities of refuge indicated his concern for the rights of the innocent against revenge. Also, man was to be judged for his motives as well as the actual act. And a system of pardoning or parole was available to mitigate the punishment of an offender.

Can a Stone Be a Witness?
(Josh. 24:26-27)

Two possible explanations might answer this question. First, the stone was a part of this earth. This earth has an intelligence and it will become a Urim and Thummim in the eternities. (D&C 130:9.) Perhaps the earth was in some way able to record the history of that event upon the rock.

Second, the stone could serve as a witness or reminder to the Israelites. As they would see the stone in later years, they would remember the earlier event. Plymouth Rock, Massachusetts, serves a similar role for many Americans today.

Judges

The book of Judges is a collection of biographical narratives combined by a later writer (probably Samuel) who joined historical events into a theological framework for the whole time period from Joshua to King Saul. The writer first reviewed some of the historical material found in Joshua, and then gave an introduction to the whole book (1:1–3:6). In the introduction he stated the framework for the collection of narratives. In the generations after Joshua, the Lord had warned the Israelites that they had not heeded his command to cleanse the land of the wicked Canaanites. Therefore he would preserve the Canaanites in the land as a snare and a test (just as he would later preserve the Lamanites with the Nephites) to see whether the Israelites would follow the Lord (2:3, 20-22).

Then the main section of the book records how twelve judges rescued later generations as they turned away from God. These judges usually tried to bring righteousness to Israel, but the people quickly reverted back to their wicked ways. Judges 2:11-19 previews this cycle, which repeated itself throughout the book:

1. The Israelites departed from the Lord and his covenant as they succumbed to the enticements of the Canaanite religion.
2. The Lord responded by turning parts of Israel over to

various enemies who harassed and subjugated the people.
3. The people cried out in their affliction and finally repented.
4. The Lord raised up a judge or deliverer who freed Israel from the oppressor.
5. The judge restored order and the land enjoyed peace during his administration. But with the death of the judge, the people quickly reverted to wickedness and idolatry.

The Israelite judges were more than military leaders and judicious administrators. (See BD "Judges.") Some composed poems in the form of songs (Deborah, 5) or riddles (Samson, 14:14, 18; 15:16) or parables (Gideon's son, Jothan, 9:8-15). Although most judges exhibited charisma, some hesitated to go into battle (Deborah, Gideon) or required promises from the people before leading them (Jephthah). One, Samson, acted without assistance from Israelite forces. One characteristic many of them shared was having the Spirit of the Lord with them (Othniel, 3:10; Deborah, a prophetess, 4:4; Gideon, 6:34; Jephthah, 11:29; Samson, 13:25; 14:6, 19; 15:14, 19). The Israelites recognized the presence of the Lord with these leaders, and even though the people were wicked they willingly followed these righteous judges (like the wicked Nephites who followed Mormon in spite of his exhortations toward their repentance; Morm. 3:1-15).

The following chart shows where the twelve judges lived and repelled the invasions from almost all of Israel's enemies from about 1250 to 1050 B.C.:

The Twelve Judges and Their Victories

1. Othniel of Judah (3:9): victory against Cushan-rishathaim.

2. Ehud of Benjamin (3:15): victory against Eglon of Moab.

3. Shamgar (3:31): victory against the Philistines.

4. Deborah of Ephraim and Barak of Naphtali (4:4-6): victory over Jabin and Sisera.

5. Gideon of Manasseh (6:11): victory over the Midianites and Amalekites.

6. Tola of Issachar (10:1).

7. Jair of Gilead (10:3).

8. Jephthah of Gilead (11:11): victory over the Ammonites.

9. Ibzan of Bethlehem (12:8).

10. Elon of Zebulun (12:11).

11. Abdon of Ephraim (12:13).

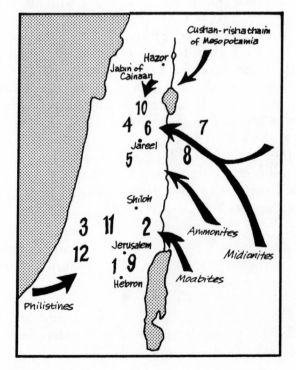

12. Samson of Dan
     (15:20): victory
     against the
     Philistines.

The last part of the book of Judges (17-21) consists of two appendixes summarizing the wicked and chaotic conditions in Israel. Whereas the introduction to the book contrasts the effective leadership of Joshua with the weakness of later generations, this conclusion to the book shows how Israelite society had degenerated even further into apostasy, priestcraft, sodomy, and civil war. In the story of Micah (17, 18), idolatry and a bribable priesthood became norms of society. During the time of the Levite and his prostitute wife (19-21), sexual abuses became so entrenched that a civil war was required to cleanse out the wicked and their defenders. One Israelite tribe, Benjamin, was almost destroyed in the process.

The spiritual framework of the whole book was one of gradually increasing wickedness. Initially the people willingly followed the Lord's prophet Joshua. Then their wickedness required external, forced humility before they followed inspired judges. Finally, their apostasy and immorality was so pervasive that the elders of Israel had to initiate a civil war before Israel lost all claims to being the people of God.

The book of Judges highlights a period of political disunity when there was no king in Israel and a time of spiritual disorganization when every person did what he thought was right. The book prepares the political and spiritual stage for the book of Samuel, which records how Israel received her first king and how Samuel became the first great prophet after Joshua. After centuries of weakness under the judges, Israel will finally be rescued from all her enemies, renewed through kingly leadership, and prepared by prophets to achieve her destiny. Studying the book of Judges shows how God worked with individuals and a whole nation to elevate them toward their divine potential even though they sought to become progressively more wicked.

Bible Dictionary references: Judges, Book of; Architecture; Baal; Benjamin; Dan; Furniture; Gideon; Grove; High Places; House; Philistines; Rain; Ras Shamrah Tablets.

Baal and Ashtart
(*Judg. 2:11-13*)

Baal and Ashtart were the main pair of gods among the Canaanites. Baal was the great male weather god, while Ashtart was the fertility goddess. Together they were responsible for the proper combination of moisture and earth and of germination and growth to ensure a successful harvest. They combined the mysteries of agriculture and sex into an apostate Canaanite religion.

Baal not only competed with Yahweh for the religious devotion of the Israelites, but was also an apostate substitute for Jehovah. According to Canaanite mythology, Baal's father was El (meaning god), the head of the gods. Baal came into power on this earth after he conquered Yamm, the dragon god of the sea (Satan?). Later, while building a temple upon this earth, Baal was killed by Mot, the god of drought, death, and the netherworld (Satan?). With help from members of his divine family, Baal was rescued from Mot, resurrected, and put on his throne. He could then join with his mother Ashtart (Ishtar or Asherah) and provide life upon the earth. Images, idols, and shrines of Baal and Ashtart (plural *Baalim* and *Ashtaroth*) were scattered throughout the land, in the "groves" and upon the "high places" where the Canaanites worshiped.

Rather than anticipating the later time when the Lord of this earth, Jehovah, would live thereon and become subject to Satan's temptations before his atonement and resurrection, the Canaanites believed that the master of the earth, Baal, had been on the earth and had already fought death (Mot). However, they also believed that Baal was not completely victorious because he still had to confront Mot each year. Indeed, Baal experienced temporary death annually and his conflict with Mot was represented on earth by the conflict waged in nature at the changes of the seasons. Baal personified spring and moisture while Mot represented the dry summer months and the drought season in Canaan. The cycles of spring and summer, fertility and drought, life and death, were all combined by the Canaanites into the story of Baal. Their religion gave them the false hope that they could control these cycles and have power to guarantee fertility of the soil. To release this power, they reenacted the life of Baal in his temple or shrine through pageantry, ritual, female idols, naked images, phallic sculptures, and religious prostitution.

Readers of the Old Testament usually assume that Baal paganism and Jehovah worship were completely different types of religion. More correctly, the Baal religion was just an apostate form of the true religion. It distorted the true relationship between God and man, it renounced the atoning powers of God, and it introduced emotional and sensual forms of worship which appeased the masses. Thus ancient Israelites faced much the same spiritual environment as modern, true believers in God do. Dominant apostate religions and worldly enticements still distract the righteous from their true purpose on earth, and each individual must still decide if he or she will serve the Lord or a form of Baal and Ashtart.

Baal   Ashtart

Deborah the Prophetess
(Judg. 4)

It seems natural to assume that a "prophetess" was simply a woman prophet. Actually, a prophetess in the Old Testament could be: (1) the wife of a prophet, (2) a woman who received prophecies of the future, or (3) someone gifted with poetical inspiration, since inspired, sacred poetry was considered to be divine. Several other prophetesses are mentioned in the Bible, such as Miriam, Hannah, Isaiah's wife, and Anna. Miriam and Deborah were probably called prophetesses because of their poetical inspiration as they developed their own special gifts of the Spirit.

The song of Deborah (Judg. 5) shows that she was a prophetess in the poetical sense. She also served as a judge who built upon her human perspectives and relied upon spiritual insight to make her decisions. She was confident in her relationship with God as evidenced in the counsel she gave Barak: "Hath not the Lord God of Israel commanded . . . ?" (Judg. 4:6.) She was a social leader and an ancient "Joan of Arc" who inspired the Israelites in battle. (Judg. 4:8.) She also demonstrated her development of the gift of prophecy. Her prophecy concerning Sisera's fate (Judg. 4:9) was fulfilled, which confirmed the fact that she did receive some knowledge of the future. All these characteristics show that Deborah was a prophetess who, as well as being poetically inspired, was also a spiritual leader of the people.

The gifts of the spirit, including prophecy, are promised to those who believe in God and follow his commandments. (Mark 16:16-18.) Paul has encouraged us to "desire spiritual gifts, but rather that ye may prophesy." (1 Cor. 14:1.) We must develop these spiritual gifts if we are to see and understand God (D&C 46:31) and if we want to witness his promised miracles, signs, and wonders (D&C 35:8). We should all be prophets or prophetesses within the areas of our own spiritual development and stewardships. Through the power of the Holy Ghost we can best receive and apply these gifts of the spirit. (D&C 46:8-28: see AF, pp. 217-18.)

Jephthah and His Daughter's Sacrifice
(Judg. 11:30-39)

Although a social outcast, Jephthah was recognized for his leadership abilities. As he confronted the Ammonites, he reviewed the biblical history of how the Israelites had conquered the Transjordan area from the Amorites, thus disproving the Ammonite claims to the land. The Ammonites still desired to control that area, and Jephthah gathered an Israelite army to repel the invasion. Before going into battle with the Spirit of the Lord upon him, Jephthah vowed that if he returned victorious he would dedicate to the Lord whatever came first out of his house to meet him. Then he added, "and I will offer it up for a burnt offering" (11:31). This promise and its fulfillment have disturbed Bible readers and confused Bible scholars for centuries.

When Jephthah returned victorious, his only child, a daughter, came out to meet him. He told her of his promise and she was willing to abide by it. She asked for a two-month period of fellowship and mourning with her friends. Then she returned to her father "who did with her according to his vow which he had vowed: and she knew no man" (11:39).

Scholars agree that she was dedicated to the Lord and that she left Jephthah's home. They disagree as to whether her dedication to the Lord comprised a lifetime of religious service (probably at the tabernacle) without the opportunity of raising a family (like being a fulltime, lifelong welfare or proselyting missionary), or the taking of her life as a burnt offering or human sacrifice.

Joseph Smith apparently did not question the Lord about this dilemma, because he made no changes in the text of his inspired translation. The story as contained in the original Hebrew is, however, ambiguous as to how the vow was to be fulfilled. The phrase "and I will offer it up for a burnt offering" (11:31) could be translated a number of ways: "and/also/but/therefore/then/or I will offer/give/ rise/lift/carry it as an offering/gift/ascent/lifting/sacrifice." It is perhaps significant that the fulfillment of this vow as recorded in verse 39 concludes with the phrase "and she knew no man." This phrase could be another way of saying "she died childless (as she was sacrificed as a burnt offering)." But it seems to mean that "she did not marry and raise a family (as she served the Lord the rest of her natural life)."

With the limited material available, and lacking revealed commentary, the answer to this dilemma is left to the individual reader. Regardless of what type of sacrifice Jephthah's daughter became, there are some positive objectives to be derived from this story:
1. Be precise and sincere when you enter any covenants with the Lord.
2. Be willing to give what is most precious to the Lord.
3. Children will be blessed eternally if they will honor and obey their parents in righteousness.
4. Absolutely fulfill any vow you make with the Lord.

Who Were the Philistines?
(*Judg. 13:1*)

The Philistines originally came from the Aegean Sea area near modern day Turkey. (See area B2 on Map 2.) Some early Philistines apparently had settled along the southeast coast of the Mediterranean Sea as early as the days of Abraham. (See Gen. 21:32, 34.) Many of them also settled in Crete (area A3 on Map 2) where they became quite numerous.

By 1200 B.C., the advancement of the Iron Age introduced from the Hittite kingdom (D2 on Map 2) and its resulting agricultural productivity (iron plows were much better than those of brass, bronze, or stone) and a population explosion as well as a major Phrygian invasion from the north pushed many Philistines from their homelands to the isles of the Mediterranean Sea and south toward Egypt and Canaan. In Egypt, they became mercenary soldiers. But as their power and numbers increased with the large migrations around 1200 B.C., the Egyptians, under Ramses III, expelled these "sea peoples" or "northerners." Many of them moved around the seacoast and settled in the rolling hills of southern Canaan. With five city-states as a power base (areas B5 and A6 on Map 6) and using their monopoly of iron instruments (1 Sam. 13:19), they attacked the Israelites from the west and sought to divide and conquer by gaining control of the Jezreel valley and the hills of Ephraim (areas C4 and C5 on Map 6). They extended their control toward the strategic territory near Shiloh, with its trade routes and highways. (1 Sam. 4.) Samson temporarily lessened their pressure upon Judah, and Samuel held them back, but it was not until the days of David that the Philistine power was finally destroyed. (See BD "Philistines.")

Samson's Covenants
(Judg. 13:5; 16:1-20)

An angel of the Lord had promised Samson's parents that their child would begin to deliver Israel from the Philistines if he would remain a Nazarite. A Nazarite was not to have strong drink, nor could he eat any fruit of the vine (grapes, raisins, etc.). He was not to have his hair cut, nor could he touch a dead person. If a person should die while the Nazarite was touching him, the Nazarite had to go through a week-long cleansing process. (Num. 6:2-12.)

As long as Samson remained faithful to his Nazarite vows, he had the strength of the Lord with him. Thus, even after his immorality in Gaza (Judg. 16:1) and his love affair with Delilah (16:4-20), he still had the strength to take down and carry city gates (16:3) and to break the bonds of strong ropes (16:12). The Lord has told us that when we do what he says, he is bound to grant us the associated blessing. And when we obtain any blessing from him it is by obedience to that law upon which it is predicated. (D&C

82:10; 130:20-21.) Samson was obeying the Nazarite vows. Thus, the Lord was bound to bless him as promised. However, Samson was disobeying other commandments and thus lost the precious blessing of the companionship of the Spirit of God. He was therefore unable to discern Delilah's true motives. Ironically, Delilah had a better sense of discernment than Samson; she could recognize when he finally told her the truth. (Judg. 16:18.) As Delilah cut Samson's hair, his vow was broken, and the Lord's power departed from him.

When a Nazarite vow or covenant was broken, it was sometimes possible to renew the vow after a period of repentance. (Num. 6:9-12.) Apparently Samson went through a period of repentance and recommitment because he again received extraordinary strength as he destroyed the Philistine temple and his own life. (Judg. 16:30.)

Tragedy came upon Samson because as he broke one commandment (morality) he lost the Spirit of the Lord. This led to his breaking other covenants and resulted in weakness, blindness, slavery, and death (both physical and spiritual).

Of What Value Was a "Piece of Silver"?
(Judg. 16:5; 17:10)

Delilah was offered 5,500 pieces of silver to deliver Samson captive to the five kings of the Philistines. The Bible does not tell us what type of coinage was used or how large these "pieces of silver" were. If they were shekels, each piece would have weighed about half an ounce and, depending upon the value of silver today, would have been worth from three to ten dollars for a total value of approximately fifteen to fifty thousand dollars in today's fluctuating money market. However, if each piece was the larger mina and not the small shekel, then each would have weighed about seventeen and one half ounces and would have been worth from one hundred fifty to five hundred dollars for a total bounty of from eight hundred thousand to almost three million dollars.

One correlation as to the relative value of these "pieces of silver" in the economy of that Israelite time period is found in the next chapter. A Levite from Bethlehem moved north to the tribal area of Ephraim and was enticed to become a personal family priest to a man named Micah (17:7-9). His yearly wages were to be an allotment of food and clothing along with "ten pieces of silver a year" (17:10). The Levite accepted these wages. Thus, if a man could receive food, clothes, and only ten pieces of silver annually for a salary, one can imagine what value and use Delilah would have made of her 5,500 pieces of silver (the wages of one man for 550 years).

Ruth

The story of Ruth occurred during the period of the judges (about 1150 B.C.) but was not written in its present form until centuries later (about 500-400 B.C.). According to early Jewish tradition as recorded in the Talmud, the story was originally written by Samuel. In its present form, it is a compact, complete literary work. It has a plot, identifiable characters, suspense, and a moral.

The plot shifts through six scenes:

1. Moab (1:1-18): Naomi, a native of Bethlehem, loses her husband and two sons before returning home with one of her daughters-in-law, Ruth.
2. Bethlehem (1:19-22): Naomi expresses deep sorrow for the emptiness of her life and the calamities which God has sent her.
3. The harvest field of Boaz (2:1-23): Ruth steps forward as the physical provider for the two women by following the Israelite custom of welfare for the poor. (See Lev. 19:9-10; Deut. 24:19-22.) Boaz recognizes her industry and grants her full harvest privileges.
4. The threshing floor of Boaz (3:1-18): Naomi instructs Ruth on how to test Boaz's intentions about marriage. Boaz is flattered and treats Ruth honorably. He accepts responsibility to clear the marriage from possible legal complications resulting from the patriarchal levirate law. (See Deut. 25:5-10; BD "Levirate Marriage.")

5. The city gates of Bethlehem (4:1-12): One other kinsman has first claim to the estate lands of Naomi and the attached moral responsibility to marry Ruth and provide her a family, but he rejects his claims. Boaz publicly claims the estate and proclaims his marriage intentions to Ruth.

6. Conclusion (4:13-17) and postscript (4:17-22): Ruth and Boaz have a son who brings joy to Naomi and who becomes an ancestor to King David (and Jesus).

Throughout the story, Naomi and Ruth faced danger in the form of drought, death, and hunger. Finally, they rested secure in the home of Boaz. More importantly, their emotional and social welfare were rewarded through their posterity. Spiritual values were also gained when God's hand in the life of this one family was made manifest. An Israelite and a Moabite had their faith rewarded and they became models for a righteous community and links in the noble heritage of David, Solomon, and Jesus. (See BD "Ruth.")

The Books of Samuel

The first book of Samuel continues the narrative of the book of Judges (review the concluding paragraphs in the article on the book of Judges in this book). Although Judges demonstrates the growing wickedness among the Israelites, the short story of Ruth indicates that there were still noble, honorable people in the land. The book of Samuel introduces new models of righteousness (Hannah, Samuel, Jonathan, David, Nathan, etc.), but it also warns us of human weaknesses (Eli, Saul, David, Ammon, Absalom, etc.). Thus, it continues the themes of both Judges and Ruth. In fact, Samuel was probably the primary editor behind all three books.

Samuel was the youthful servant of Eli, the high priest, and later became the prophet, seer, and judge of Israel. He bridged a crucial time period as Israel changed from a loose confederation of tribes under the leadership of elders and judges to a monarchy under the rule of Saul and then David. The lives of these three men, Samuel, Saul, and David, dominate the books of Samuel, which record the following events:

1 Samuel
I. Life and administration of Samuel (1-12).
    A. Inspired promise, youth, prophetic call (1-3).
    B. Ark of the covenant and the Philistines (4-6).
    C. Samuel leads and teaches Israel (7).

   D. Desires for and dangers of a king (8).
   E. Saul to be a "prince over Israel" (9-10:16).
   F. Saul's inhibitions (10:17-27).
   G. Saul exhibits leadership (11).
   H. Samuel's last message and warning (12).

II. Saul as king (13-31).
   A. Saul vacillates between strength and weakness (13-15).
   B. David's anointing, victory over Goliath, interactions with Saul's family (16-20).
   C. Saul seeks David's life (21-24).
   D. David's friends and refuge among the Philistines (25-27).
   E. Saul's discouragement, defeat, and death (28-31).

2 Samuel
I. The kingship of David (1-24).
   A. David consolidates rule and conquers Jerusalem (1-6).
   B. Promises to David and his family (7).
   C. David's strong rule (8-10).
   D. David and Bathsheba (11-12).
   E. David loses spirit of leadership (13-21, 24).
      1. Family problems (13-18).
      2. Political problems: Disobedience by generals and civil war (18-20).
      3. Natural catastrophies: Famine and pestilence (21, 24).
   F. David's last words—a psalm and a prayer (22-23).

A number of important lessons can be learned from these stories: the Lord answers prayers (of Hannah, David), the importance of religious leaders and their families in setting a good example (Eli and his sons, Samuel's sons), the calling of a young prophet (Samuel), having trust in the Lord (ark of the covenant and the Philistines), the dangers of centralized rule (Israel desires a king), the value of personal integrity and discipline (Saul's problems in his relationship with God), a young man grows in favor with the Lord (David), the evils of jealousy (Saul), trust in the Lord during periods of persecution (David), power and promises to the righteous (David), danger of evil thoughts and acts (David and Bathsheba), the frustrations of life without the Spirit of God (David), and the need to account for stewardships before death (Samuel and David).

In other words, there is a wealth of stories, moral lessons, gospel themes, historical facts, and personality insights in these chapters. For the first time since the life of Moses, the Old Testament record has slowed down a little and given us more material covering just a short time period with enough facts to study characters, events, and feelings in greater depth. The books of Samuel are a record deserving careful study. The footnotes and topical guide references in the LDS edition of the Bible help clarify this material so that its richness can be appreciated.

Bible Dictionary references: Samuel; Samuel, Books of; Anoint; Dagon; David; Eli; Emerods; Giants; Jerusalem; Prophet; Saul; Seer; Shiloh; Sling; Zadok.

Studying a Prophet's Message
(1 Sam. 3:19-21)

At an early age, Samuel was recognized and respected as a prophet. Other prophets, such as Moses and Amos, were adults before they received their prophetic callings. Many prophets were respected by the Israelites, but others, like Jeremiah, were abused.

The background of a prophet often affected his relationship with the people and the way he delivered God's messages. Of more importance were the people's religious attitudes and receptiveness.

Some of the messages from the prophets were not recorded, or if recorded they were not passed on, so that we may read their names and some of their words, but much more has been lost. (See BD "Lost Books.")

The Old Testament reader must study the remaining

available records and try to understand and relate to the material. To better appreciate the histories and records of these prophets, it might be helpful to evaluate each of them in light of the following ten questions:

The Prophet
1. What was his personal preparation (including foreordination) for his prophetic calling?
2. How was his calling received and how was his role outlined by the Lord?

The Message
3. What was the means of his reception of messages from the Lord (dreams, visions, angels, etc.)?
4. What was his comprehension of the message and its application?
5. In his deliverance of God's word, how much was he required to pass on and in what form did he give it?

The Record
6. What was the reaction of the people to the message and the prophet?
7. Who made a record of the prophet's words and in what form?
8. How well were the prophetic writings preserved, and how good is the translation we use to study them?

The Meaning
9. What meaning did the prophet's own audience attach to his words?
10. What application can we gain from the prophet's words for us today?

These questions could also be asked about our contemporary prophets and their messages. And as we answer these questions about the Old Testament prophetic writings, we could also evaluate how well we individually are preparing ourselves to receive the word of the Lord, how effective we are in delivering it (to our family, classes, friends, etc.), and how it is being received and recorded.

David Runs from Saul
(1 Sam. 19-27)

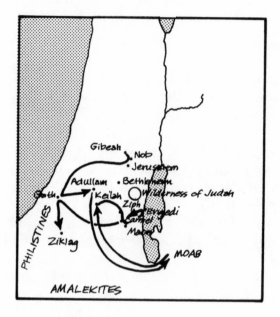

David's Wars
(2 Sam. 8, 10, 12, 21)

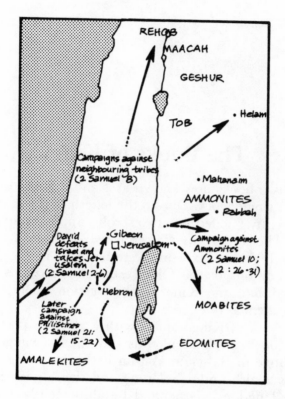

REHOB

MAACAH

GESHUR

TOB

• Helam

Campaigns against
neighbouring tribes
(2 Samuel 8)

• Mahanaim

AMMONITES

• Rabbah

David
defeats
Israel and
takes Jer-
usalem
(2 Samuel 2-6)

• Gibeon

□ Jerusalem

Campaign against
Ammonites
(2 Samuel 10;
12 : 26 - 31)

Later
campaign
against
Philistines
(2 Samuel 21:
15-22)

• Hebron

MOABITES

EDOMITES

AMALEKITES

The Books of Kings

The two books now known as 1 and 2 Kings originally formed a single work. Due to the length of the material, it was anciently divided into two scrolls, approximately equal in size. The formal division into two separate books was completed by the sixteenth century A.D. in the Hebrew printed editions of the Old Testament, and this pattern continued into the King James Version. Here, we will consider them as one book.

The book of Kings opens with a glorious portrayal of King Solomon's reign and ends with the last king of Judah as a captive in Babylon. Within its history, we see Israel reach its zenith under Solomon and then divide into two separate kingdoms, Israel and Judah, which both fall into wickedness before their destruction and captivity by Mesopotamian powers.

First we see the northern kingdom of Israel follow prophetic promises and the leadership of Jeroboam to break away from the southern tribes. Within two dynamic centuries, Israel rises to power and influence, struggles with changing dynasties, sinks into moral corruption (especially under Ahab and Jezebel), and then experiences a brief burst of glory under Jeroboam II before being destroyed by the Assyrians in 721 B.C.

We also see the smaller, weaker southern kingdom of Judah consolidate its rule under the house of David to seek its own power and independence. Its relationship with Israel sometimes draws the two nations together, but it usually weakens both as they compete and even war with each other.

In the century after Israel's destruction, Judah stands alone against the Assyrians, experiences worse moral corruption (under wicked King Manasseh), and attempts a religious revival under King Josiah, but is so weakened that it becomes a political pawn of Babylon and Egypt until the Babylonians destroy its capital and temple during 587-586 B.C.

The book of Kings is more than the historical review of the rise and fall of Israelite nations. In its pages we also observe individuals struggling for higher and nobler ideals against religious and political obstacles. Elijah confronts the priests of Baal supported by the Tyrian princess Jezebel. Kings contend against neighboring nations and Mesopotamian powers. Elisha and later prophets struggle against religious indifference, immorality, and selfishness. Good and bad kings, weak and strong leaders, charismatic and mild prophets interact with each other through centuries of Israelite history and provide us with personality insights, historical backgrounds, literary masterpieces, and above all an understanding of God's involvement with the chosen family of Jacob. We see how the Lord warns and chastens Israel and Judah, and how they disregard the warnings until complete destruction comes upon them. We need to turn to the prophetic literature (especially Isaiah and Jeremiah) of the same time period to appreciate the promises of a Messiah and of an eventual restoration and blessings that would later come to the descendants of these defeated Israelite nations. (See TG "Israel, Gathering of.") The book of Kings only briefly mentions the promises of their repentance and forgiveness (see 1 Kgs. 8:46-53) as it records their downfall.

An unknown editor or compiler used a number of records to complete this work. He probably lived during the reign of Jehoiachin, one of the last kings of Judah, and

finished this book by 590 B.C. He mentioned at least three
major sources for his material: the Acts of Solomon (1 Kgs.
11:41), and the books of the chronicles of the kings of Israel
(1 Kgs. 14:19) and of Judah (1 Kgs. 14:29). Records of
Ahab (1 Kgs. 20, 22), Elijah (1 Kgs. 17-19, 21; 2 Kgs. 1),
Elisha (2 Kgs. 2-8, 13) Isaiah (2 Kgs. 18-20), and the
temple (2 Kgs. 12, 16, 23), may have also been used.

The compiler followed the pattern of other ancient his-
torians. He used available records, selected the desired
material, and added his own commentary and those additional items which he felt were essential. After his record of
Solomon's reign and the division of Israel and Judah, he
developed a pattern or framework to tell the story of almost
all the kings. First he gave an opening formula (in which
were given the date the reign began, its length, the syn-
chronism with the king of the other kingdom, and, in the
case of the Judean kings, the name of the king's mother);
next came his judgment or religious evaluation of the king
in question (such as, "And he [Hezekiah] did right in the
sight of the Lord, according to all that David his father
did." 2 Kgs. 18:3); then followed various extracts from the
sources and other records; and finally came his closing
formula (indicating which records contained further information and recording the king's death, place of burial, and
successor's name). The compiler followed this pattern in all
cases except for the last king of his record, Jehoiachin, and
those kings who were either assassinated or deposed and
who were usually not given a proper or state burial.

The book of Kings divides easily into three major
sections:

I.   Solomon's Reign (1-11).
     A. Last days of David and Solomon's accession (1, 2).
     B. Solomon and his glory (3-11).
II. The divided kingdom, Israel and Judah (1 Kgs. 12–
     2 Kgs. 17).
     A. Division and reigns of Jeroboam and Rehoboam
        (12-14).

B. Synchronistic history of Israel and Judah (15, 16).
C. Ahab and the fall of the house of Omni (1 Kgs. 17–2 Kgs. 10).
   1. Elijah's ministry (1 Kgs. 17–2 Kgs. 2:11).
   2. Elisha's ministry (2 Kgs. 2:12–13:21).
   3. Jehu's revolt, death of Jezebel, and destruction of Ahab's family (9, 10).
D. Synchronistic history of Israel and Judah until the fall of Israel to Assyria (11-17).

III. The kingdom of Judah alone (18-25).
  A. Reign of good King Hezekiah (18-20).
  B. Wicked King Manasseh (21).
  C. Reformation of Josiah (22-23:30).
  D. Disruption and destruction of Judah (23:31–25:30).

The compiler of the book of Kings is sometimes called the "Deuteronomistic writer" because of the religious message that his "historical" book presented. Shortly before the writer compiled his material, King Josiah of Judah had initiated a major religious reform and temple renovation. While cleaning the temple storerooms, workers found a scroll of the book of Deuteronomy. Most religious records and sacred writings had earlier been destroyed by the wicked King Manasseh. The reading of this recovered book of Deuteronomy to King Josiah demonstrated how far Judah had departed from the law of Moses. Deuteronomy chapters 27 and 28 clearly indicated the blessings of obedience and the curses of disobedience to the Sinai covenant. The compiler of the book of Kings observed the fulfillment of these Deuteronomistic promises and emphasized the patterns of obedience or disobedience and of blessings or curses which characterized the period of Israelite kings. Like Mormon extracting, compiling, and commenting on the large plates of Nephi (which contained a secular history), the compiler of the book of Kings used secular historical records to demonstrate how the kings' and people's religious behavior had affected their military and political

conditions. The writer did not distort history, but he reviewed it within the context of the broader dimensions of
God-man relationships. A modern Old Testament scholar,
Brevard S. Childs, has evaluated the compiler's use of
historical sources:

> It is evident that the books of Kings represent only a skeletal
> account of a history which extends from the accession of Solomon to the
> destruction of Jerusalem in 587. A most striking feature is the conscious
> principle of selection which is operative throughout the books. Not only
> is the reader continually told where he can find additional information
> about each king ('now the rest of the acts of N . . . are they not written
> in the book of the . . .'), but also there is no attempt whatever to give a
> detailed account of each king's reign. The obvious lack of concern for a
> detailed survey would confirm the conclusion that the writer's purpose
> in the history lay elsewhere. Several indices reveal the author's true
> intention. First of all, the writer makes it clear that he conceives of his
> task as describing a unified history of events of one people within a
> circumscribed period. In spite of the political division into two king-
> doms the writer refuses to treat them separately, but shuttles back and
> forth between them. The history ends with the loss of the land and the
> exile of the people. However, the threat of this disaster appears from the
> beginning of the history and connects the various reigns like a red
> thread. The writer continually recapitulates prior events and adum-
> brates future ones in order to enforce his theological interpretation of
> the whole history as a unified entity.
>
> Secondly, the writer's consistent attempt to offer reasons for the
> impending judgment further confirms his intention to explain as well as
> to describe why Israel was destroyed. Sometimes he uses a stereotyped
> expression to characterize a reign ('he did not turn from the sins of
> Jeroboam', II Kings 3.1; 10.28; 13.2, etc.), but at other times he reveals
> an essential feature of his composition by assigning a lengthy theologi-
> cal explanation to justify the divine judgment (1 Kings 11.9ff.; II Kings
> 17.7ff.). The author's concern to see an inner connection between the
> various epochs of Israel's history sets his work apart from the various
> sources which he had at his disposal.
>
> The manner in which the reader is constantly referred back to the
> writer's sources indicates that he did not envision his composition to be
> in contradiction with his sources. He was not attempting to rewrite
> history nor to supply hitherto unknown information. Neither was he
> writing a 'theological history' which operated on its own principles
> apart from the history found in the official records. Event and interpre-
> tation belonged together and he needed only a selection from a larger
> historical sequence to demonstrate his thesis. (Brevard S. Childs, *Intro-
> duction to the Old Testament as Scripture* [Philadelphia: Fortress Press,
> 1979], pp. 288-89.)

The book of Kings is not a "historical" work according to the modern definition of that term. The compiler of the book did not write history as much as he illustrated how the hand of the Lord could be seen in the historical events of ancient Israel. Of greatest historical value are the selections and excerpts from earlier records that he included, often in their original form, in his work. Of weakest historical validity are the chronological dates he used. The different earlier records which he used apparently had their own unique dating systems. As he recorded the chronological data from the different sources, he simply listed the dates and did not attempt to correlate them with the other sources.

In spite of these deficiencies, the book of Kings provides a historical record of this time period that is more accurate, complete, and enlightening than any other history of the same age. The book also provides us with insights into the lives of the prophets Elijah and Elisha. It gives us historical background and some information about the lives of other great prophets, such as Jonah, Amos, Hosea, Micah, Isaiah, Zephaniah, Jeremiah, Lehi, Nahum, and Habakkuk. More importantly, the book of Kings shows us how God dealt with the children of Israel. Perhaps we can recognize similar patterns and warnings in our society, as we modern children of Israel strive to honor and represent him in an increasingly wicked world.

Bible Dictionary references:

1 Kings: Kings, Books of; Ahab; Asa; Bethel; Calves; Elias; Elijah; Idol; Israel, Kingdom of; Jeroboam; Judah, Kingdom of; Rehoboam; Schools of the Prophets; Solomon; Temple; Temple of Solomon.

2 Kings: Assyria; Babylon; Captivities of the Israelites; Commerce; Diaspora; Dispersion; Elisha; Hezekiah; Hezekiah's Tunnel; Jew; Josiah; Molech; Samaritans; Ship.

Solomon's Temple
(1 Kgs. 8)

Prophets and Their Prophecies in Israel and Judah from the Time of Solomon to Elijah
(1 Kgs. 11-18)

I. Ahijah, the Shilonite.
  A. Prophecy of the division of the kingdom. (1 Kgs. 11:26-40.)
     Solomon's servant, Jeroboam, was stopped on the road by Ahijah.
     Prophecy:
       1. Because of idolatry, the kingdom of Solomon would be divided, with Jeroboam the ruler over ten tribes.
       2. The kingdom would be divided in the days of Solomon's son.
       3. This son would rule one tribe and Jerusalem.
     Fulfillment:
       1 Kings 12:1-20; 2 Chronicles 10:1-19.
  B. Prophecy of the fall of the house of Jeroboam. (1 Kgs. 14:1-16.)
     Jeroboam sent his wife in disguise to Ahijah in

Shiloh to determine if his son would die.
Prophecy:
1. The house of Jeroboam would be destroyed by a new king.
2. Jeraboam's relatives who died in the city would be eaten by dogs; those who died in the fields would be eaten by birds.
3. The son would die, and would be the only descendant of Jeroboam who would be buried in a grave.
4. Israel would be rooted up and scattered beyond the river.

Fulfillment:
1 Kings 14:17-18; 15:25-30; 2 Kings 18:9-12.

II. Shemaiah, the man of God.
   A. Judah not to attack Israel. (1 Kgs. 12:21-24; 2 Chr. 11:1-4.)
   Rehoboam with 180,000 men wanted to attack Israel and restore it to his kingdom.
   Lord's message:
   Do not fight your brethren in Israel, as the division was caused by the Lord.
   Result:
   Rehoboam hearkened unto the Lord's counsel.
   B. Shishak's attack upon Judah. (2 Chr. 12:1-8.)
   Pharaoh Shishak of Egypt attacked Judah.
   Prophecy:
   1. Because of Judah's wickedness, it would fall to Shishak. However, the princes of Judah would then humble themselves.
   2. Judah would not be destroyed.
   3. She would become the servant of Egypt.
   Fulfillment:
   2 Chronicles 12:9-12.

III. A man of God from Judah.

A. Bones of pagan priests would be burned by Josiah. (1 Kgs. 13:1-10.)

The man of God prophesied to the pagan altar which Jeroboam had built in Bethel.

Prophecy:

1. A child by the name of Josiah would be born into the house of David.
2. He would burn pagan priests' and men's bones upon that altar.
3. As a sign, the altar would be rent and the ashes poured out.

Fulfillment:

The sign was given immediately. (1 Kgs. 13:5.) Josiah came about three hundred years later. (2 Kgs. 23:15-20; 2 Chr. 34:3-7.)

IV. An old prophet in Bethel.

A. The man of God of Judah killed for disobedience. (1 Kgs. 13:11-32.)

The man of God of Judah told not to eat or drink in Bethel. An angel appeared to an old prophet in Bethel and told him to have the man of God come back to his (the old prophet's) house in Bethel to eat and drink, that the angel might prove the man of God (JST). The man of God returned to Bethel and broke his fast.

Prophecy:

Because the man of God disobeyed the Lord, his carcass would not come into the sepulcher of his fathers.

Fulfillment:

1 Kings 13:23-32; 2 Kings 23:17-18.

V. Azariah, the son of Obed.

A. God will reward Judah. (2 Chr. 15:1-8.)

Asa (third King of Judah) had been righteous.

Prophecy:

As long as Asa relied on the Lord and re-

membered him, the Lord would bless Asa and Judah and there would be peace.
Fulfillment:
2 Chronicles 15:9-19; see next prophecy.

VI.   Hanai, the seer.
   A. Judah to have wars. (2 Chr. 16:1-10.)
   Asa bribed Syria to attack Israel, which was fortifying her border against Judah.
   Prophecy:
      1. Since Asa and Judah had relied upon the king of Syria instead of the Lord, Syria would be out of Judah's control.
      2. Asa and Judah would have wars from thenceforth.
   Fulfillment:
      1 Kings 22:29-32; 2 Kings 8:25-28; 16:5; 2 Chronicles 28:5-15.

VII. Jehu, son of Hanai.
   A. The end of the house of Baasha. (1 Kgs. 16:1-7.)
   Baasha (Israel's third king) had destroyed the house of Jeroboam, but he continued in idolatry.
   Prophecy:
      The Lord would destroy his house as he did Jeroboam's, and his posterity would be eaten by dogs and fowls.
   Fulfillment:
      1 Kings 16:8-13.
   B. Reproof upon Jehoshaphat. (2 Chr. 19:2-3.)
   Jehoshaphat (Judah's fourth king) had allied himself with Ahab of Israel in a war with Syria.
   Prophecy:
      1. Why do you help the ungodly and love them that hate the Lord (i.e., the Israelites)—the wrath of God is upon you.
      2. Nevertheless, there is good in you as you prepare your heart to seek God.

Fulfillment:
Jehoshaphat went among his people and
caused them to return to God. (2 Chr. 19:4-
11.)

VIII. Micaiah, the son of Imba.
A. Evil would come upon Ahab and the kingdom of
Israel. (2 Chr. 18:1-27.)
Ahab sought support from false prophets to fight
against Syria; his ally, Jehoshaphat of Judah,
requested counsel from a prophet of God.
Prophecy:
1. Israel's soldiers would be scattered.
2. Ahab would not return in peace (alive).
Fulfillment:
Ahab disguised himself but was still killed in
a losing battle. (2 Chr. 18:28-34.)

IX.   One hundred prophets in Israel. (1 Kgs. 18:4, 13.)
Jezebel, the wife of Ahab (Israel's seventh king),
sought to have all the prophets of Jehovah killed; but
Obadiah, the king's servant, saved one hundred of
them in two caves; therefore, there were many
"prophets" at the same time.

Divided Kingdoms

Year B.C.	Prophets	Kings of Israel	Kings of Judah	Prophets
		Jeroboam I (930-909)	Rehoboam (930-913)	
		Nadab (909-908)	Abijam (913-911)	
900		Baasha (908-886)	Asa (911-870)	
		Elah and Zimri (886-885)		

Omri
(885-874)

Jehoshaphat
(873-848)*

Elijah	Ahab	
(870-850)	(874-853)	
	Ahaziah	
	(853-852)	Jehoram
Elisha	Joram	(853-841)
(850-795)	(Jehoram)	Ahaziah
	(852-841)	(841)
	Jehu	Athaliah
	(841-814)	(841-835)
		Joash
		(835-796)
	Jehoahaz	
	(814-798)	
800 Jonah	Joash	Amaziah
(780-760?)	(Jehoash)	(796-767)
	(798-782)	
	Jeroboam II	Uzziah
	(787-746)*	(Azariah)
		(791-740)*
Amos		
(765-750)		
Hosea		
(755-720)		

Zechariah		Isaiah	
(746-745)		(740-690)	
Shallum		Micah	
(745)		(739-695)	
Menahem	Jotham		
(745-736)	(750-735)*		
Pekahiah			
(736-735)			

	Pekah (751-732)†	Ahaz (743-720)**	
721 Fall of Israel	Hosea (732-722)		
		Hezekiah (728-692)*	
700			
		Manasseh (696-642)*	
		Amon (642-640)	Zephaniah (640-620)
		Josiah (640-609)	
			Jeremiah (625-580)
		Jehoahaz (609)	Nahum (620-600?)
		Jehoiakim (609-597)	
			Habakkuk (605-580?)
600			
		Jehoiachin (597)	
		Zedekiah (597-587)	
587-586 Fall of Jerusalem			

*Indicates that this king served early period of some years as a co-regent or acting king, usually with his father. Thus, the reigns of two (**or even three) kings would overlap.

†Pekah was a rebel king in the area east of the Jordan River during most of this period (751-735).

Elijah's Travels
(1 Kgs. 18, 19; 2 Kgs. 2)

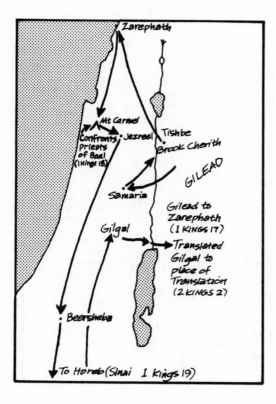

Elisha's Travels
(2 Kgs. 2-4, 8)

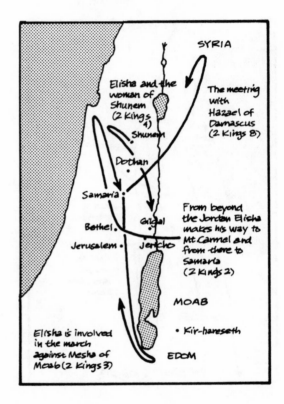

Power of Elisha
(2 Kgs. 2:9-13)

Although often considered in the shadow of Elijah, his disciple Elisha was a prophet in his own right who performed a number of miracles and gave numerous prophecies. Among those recorded are:

Miracles

1. Parted waters of Jordan (2:14).
2. Healed springs near Jericho (2:22).
3. Commanded two she bears (2:24).
4. Water in Edom (3:20).
5. Multiplied oil (4:6).
6. Brought child back from death (4:35).
7. Cured poisonous food (4:41).
8. Multiplied food (4:43).
9. Healed Naman of leprosy (5:14).
10. Pronounced leprosy upon Gehazi (5:27).
11. Floated iron ax head (6:6).
12. Blinded Syrian army (6:18).
13. Caused Syrian army to flee (7:7).
14. Man restored to life after touching Elisha's bones (13:21).

Prophecies

1. Told men of Jericho they could not find Elijah (2:18).
2. Israel would defeat Moab (3:18, 25).
3. Promised barren woman a child (4:17).
4. Told Israel how to avoid Syrian army (6:8-11).
5. Foretold personal visit by king of Israel (6:32).
6. Foretold time of plenty on following day during a time of famine (7:1, 16).
7. Promised a man an unusual death within a day (7:2, 17).

8. Foretold seven-year drought (8:1).
9. Told king of Syria he would not recover from a disease (8:10).
10. Promised and foreordained king of Syria(9:3; 10:11).
11. Foretold how many times Israel would be victorious over Syria (13:19).

History of the Palestine Area, 760-690 B.C.

Judah	*Israel*	*Assyria (and Syria)*
760: Uzziah (or Azariah, 791-740) has served as co-regent (791-771) and king of Judah since he was sixteen years old. (2 Kgs. 15:1-4; 2 Chr. 26:1-15.)	760: Jeroboam II (787-746) has served as co-regent (787-782) and then expands Israel's borders and influence to their greatest extent since Solomon's time. (2 Kgs. 14:23-29.)	760: Ashur-dan III (772-755) and Ashur-Nirari V (754-745) continue a period of Assyrian decline and weakness; one of these kings probably ruled greater Ninevah during Jonah's visit and then called upon his people to repent. (Jonah 3:4; 2 Kgs. 14:25; Matt. 12:40, 41.)
c. 760-740: Amos and Hosea serve as prophets and warn Israel of her wickedness and pending destruction.	751: Pekah (751-732) sets himself up as a rebel king in the Transjordan (area east of Jordan River).	
750: Uzziah tries to burn incense in the temple and becomes leprous; his son Jotham (750-735) acts as co-regent or king. (2 Chr. 26:16-23;	746: Jeroboam's son, Zechariah (746-745), rules for six months before he is murdered by Shallum, who	745: Tiglath-Pileser III (745-727, called Pul in the Bible) becomes king, subjects Babylon, and begins em-

2 Kgs. 15:5, 32-38.)

743: Ahaz begins to serve as "crown-prince" or co-regent with his father Jotham, while his grandfather, Uzziah, was a leper.

740: King Uzziah dies, and Isaiah has great vision. (Isa. 6.)

735: Jotham finishes his strong reign (2 Chr. 27) and his son Ahaz (735-720) begins wicked rule and then is invaded from the north; he seeks Assyrian aid against Isaiah's advice. (2 Chr. 28; 2 Kgs. 16; Isa. 7.)

rules for one month before he is slain by Menahem (745-736), who rules Samaria for ten years. (2 Kgs. 15:8-18.)

c. 740: Israel pays tribute to Assyria. (2 Kgs. 15:19-22.)

736: Menahem's son, Pekahial (736-735) rules for two years before being murdered by Pekah, who then rules all of Israel (Samaria and Transjordan) for four years. (2 Kgs. 15:23-28.)

732: Hoshea (732-722) slays Pekah and establishes pro-Assyrian policy.

pire expansion to Egypt on the west and the Indus River (India) on the east.

740: Rezin (740-732) becomes king of Syria.

735: Rezin and Pekah form a Syro-Israelite alliance and attempt to get other neighboring countries to join them in fighting against Assyria. They invade Judah to force her support, but Ahaz decides to favor Assyria.

732: Tiglath-Pileser III (Pul) destroys Syria, slays Rezin, and invades Israel,

(2 Kgs. 15:30;
17:1-3.)

taking many
captives. (2 Kgs.
15:29; 16:9.)

Micah and
Isaiah denounce
Ahaz.

730-727: Pul con-
quers and an-
nexes Trans-
jordan, deporting
a large part of
the population
(including por-
tions of Israelite
tribes of Manas-
seh, Gad, and
Reuben).

728: Hezekiah
begins to serve
as a co-regent
with his father,
Ahaz. (2 Kgs.
18:1.)

727: Hezekiah,
as acting ruler,
initiates strong
religious reforms.
(2 Chr. 29;
2 Kgs. 18:3-8;
Num. 21:4-9.)

c. 726: Hoshea
refuses to pay
Assyrian tribute
and seeks
Egyptian
alliance.

726: Shalmaneser
V (726-722) be-
gins reign and
invades Israel,
besieges Samaria
for three years
and takes ten
tribes captive.
(2 Kgs. 17:4-6;
18:9-12.)

722: Wicked
Israel falls to the
Assyrians. Over
27,000 Israelites
exiled to north-
east Assyria.
Other settlers in
Samaria inter-
marry with re-
maining Israel-
ites and become
the semi-pagan
Samaritans. (2

720: Ahaz dies
and Isaiah urges
on Hezekiah
(720-692) in his
radical religious
reforms. (2
Chr. 30, 31.)

721: Sargon II
(721-705) com-
pletes conquest
of Samaria and
destroys the
kingdom of
Israel.

c. 707: Hezekiah's

712: Sargon II
travels down the

sickness and gifts from Babylon. (Isa. 38, 39; 2 Kgs. 20.)

Kgs. 17:7-41.)

seacoast west of Judah, besieges Ashdod, and forces the Egyptian twenty-fifth (or Ethiopian) Dynasty to open trade relations with Assyria.

705: Sargon II slain in battle, his son, Sennacherib (704-681) begins powerful reign; he receives temple tribute from Hezekiah. (2 Kgs. 18:13-16.)

701: Sennacherib's generals besiege Jerusalem and employ psychological warfare; Hezekiah's tunnel, Isaiah's counsel, and a plague from the Lord preserve Judah. (2 Chr. 32; 2 Kgs. 18:17-36; 19:1-37; Isa. 36, 37.)

696: Perhaps because of Hezekiah's ill health (he died about 692) Manasseh (696-642) begins co-regency at the tender age of twelve. He quickly establishes a strong pagan and perverse policy (2 Chr. 33:1-9; 2 Kgs. 21:1-18); although he may have repented somewhat in his later years (2 Chr. 33:10-20). However, according to Jewish traditions, he slew many of the prophets and had Isaiah encased in a tree trunk and sawn asunder with a wooden saw. Some Jewish traditions also state that Hezekiah's wife was Isaiah's daughter—if true then Isaiah would have been killed by his own grandson.

Assyrian Invasions
(2 Kgs. 15-19)

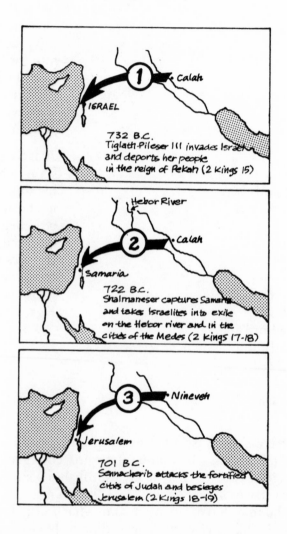

1 • Calah

ISRAEL

732 B.C.
Tiglath-Pileser III invades Israel
and deports her people
in the reign of Pekah (2 Kings 15)

Hebor River

2 • Calah

• Samaria

722 B.C.
Shalmaneser captures Samaria
and takes Israelites into exile
on the Hebor river and in the
cities of the Medes (2 Kings 17-18)

3 • Nineveh

• Jerusalem

701 B.C.
Sennacherib attacks the fortified
cities of Judah and besieges
Jerusalem (2 Kings 18-19)

Assyrian Provinces in Palestine
(2 Kgs. 18)

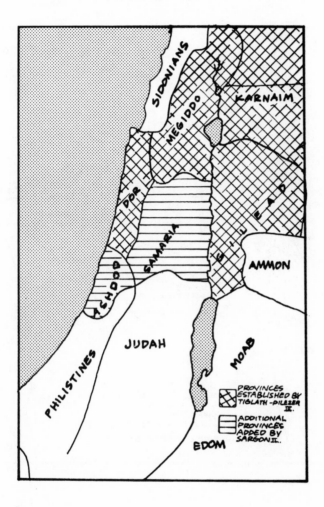

Sennacherib's Attack
(2 Kgs. 18-19)

History of the Palestine Area, 690-580 B.C.

Year B.C.	Judah	Year B.C.	Babylon (and Middle East)
690	Manasseh (696-642) develops strong pagan rule, offers own son as human sacrifice, kills innocent people—even the prophets (2 Kgs. 21:1-18; 2 Chr. 33:1-20), pays taxes to Assyria, supports Assyrian armies against the Egyptians; according to tradition he also has religious records and their possessors burned by fire.		Sennacherib (704-681) rules strong Assyrian Empire. Esarhaddon (680-669) rules Assyria.
		663	Asshurbanapal (668-627) rules Assyria, sacks Egypt (especially Thebes).
642	Amon (642-640), Manasseh's son, rules until assassinated by his servants. (2 Kgs. 21:19-26: 2 Chr. 33:21-25.)		
640	Josiah (640-609) begins reign.		
?	Zephaniah (between 640-620) prophesies a "great" day against Judah. (Zeph. 1:1, 14.)		
?	Nahum (c. 630-615) prophesies against Ninevah.	632	Scythian invasion weakens Assyria.

628   Josiah begins some re-
        ligious reforms. (2 Chr.
        34:3-7.)

627   Jeremiah (627-580) be-
        gins to prophesy. (Jer.   626   Nabopolassar (626-
        1:2.)   605), resurgent
                                              Babylonian king, and
622   Deuteronomic reform   Median attacks weaken
        stimulated by discovery   Assyria, Judah left
        of Torah scroll during   alone.
        temple cleansing. (2
        Kgs. 22:1–23:28; 2 Chr.   612   Ninevah falls to Medes
        34:8–35:19.)   and Babylonians.

                                      610   Haran falls to Babylo-
                                              nians

609   Josiah killed at   609   Death of Assyrian em-
        Megiddo in futile at-   pire as Assyrian-
        tempt to stop Egyptian   Egyptian coalition de-
        army. (2 Kgs. 23:29,   feated in attempt to
        30; 2 Chr. 35:20-27.)   regain Haran.

609   Jehoahaz (609) rules   Pharaoh Necho II
        three months before   (610-594) controls
        deportation to Egypt by   Palestine area, but
        Necho. (2 Kgs. 23:31-   gradually loses control
        33; 2 Chr. 36:1-3.)   to the Babylonians.

609   Jehoiakim (609-598)
        pays tribute to Egypt.
        (2 Kgs. 23: 34-37; 2
        Chr. 36:4-8.)

c. 608 Urijah, a prophet, is
        slain for testifying de-
        struction to Judah.
        (Jer. 26:1, 20-23.)

605   Daniel and selected   605   Babylonians defeat
        youths taken to Baby-   Egyptians at Car-
        lon. (Dan. 1:1-4.)   chemish and control
                                              Judah.

605? Habbakuk (605-598?)
questions God about
Israelite wickedness
and Babylonian power
over Judah.

602? Judah invaded by
marauding bands. (2
Kgs. 24:2; Jer. 9:10-22;
12: 7-13.)

598 Jehoiachin (598-597)
rules three months until
mid-March, when he
and 10,000 Jews (in-
cluding Ezekiel) taken
in first deportation to
Babylon. (2 Kgs. 24:1-
16; 2 Chr. 36:9, 10.)

597 Zedekiah (597-587)
rules Judah. (2 Kgs.
24:17-20; 2 Chr.
36:11-21.)

597 Lehi receives a sign and
a vision and begins to
prophesy. (1 Ne. 1:4-
15, 18-20.)

589 Lehi's family arrives at
Bountiful; builds ship.
(1 Ne. 17:4-14.)

587 Jerusalem falls to the
Babylonians after
eighteen-month siege;
Solomon's temple de-
stroyed; Jeremiah res-
cued from slave gangs
as second deportation

603 Nebuchadnessar (605-
562, powerful Babylo-
nian king, has dream
interpreted by Daniel
(Dan. 2:1, 19-45).

592 Ezekiel begins to prophesy
(Ezek. 1:2, 3).

588 Nebuchadnessar again
invades Judah and be-
sieges Jerusalem.

? Shadrach, Meschach,
and Abednego cast into
the fiery furnace and
preserved. (Dan. 3.)

goes to Babylon. (2
Kgs. 25:1-21; Jer.
39:1-14; 52:1-29.)

582   Babylonian-appointed
governor, Gedaliah, as-
sassinated; many Jews
take Jeremiah and flee
to Egypt; other Jews
taken in third deporta-
tion to Babylon. (2
Kgs. 25:22-26; Jer.
40:1–43:7; 52:30.)

580?   Obadiah (c. 586-570)
prophesies to Edom
and about the last days.

580   Jeremiah prophesies to
the Jews in Egypt. (Jer.
43:8–44:30.)

570?   Jeremiah stoned to
death by Jews in Egypt
(according to tradition;
other traditions have
him and some of
Zedekiah's daughters
immigrating to the
British Isles).

The Last Kings of Judah

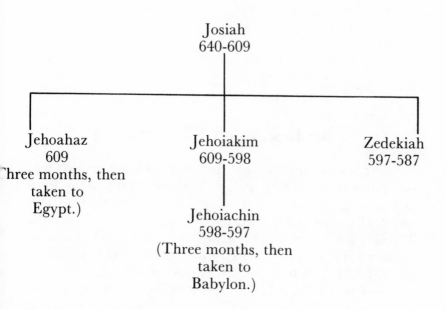

Josiah
640-609

Jehoahaz
609
(Three months, then
taken to
Egypt.)

Jehoiakim
609-598

Jehoiachin
598-597
(Three months, then
taken to
Babylon.)

Zedekiah
597-587

The Books of Chronicles

Like Samuel and Kings, this work has been divided into two parts, 1 and 2 Chronicles. It shares many other similarities with Samuel and Kings, as they both provided much of the material used by the writer of these records. The Chronicles contain the genealogy and historical outline of the righteous generations of man from the time of Adam to the fall of Judah in 587 B.C. Thus, they duplicate (often word-for-word) material found in Genesis, Samuel, and Kings. It is helpful to read Chronicles after having studied these earlier works. Chronicles thus serves as a review, but it also provides some additional facts as it describes the events and persons. It also gives some new, unique information. The following chapters or portions of chapters contain material not found outside Chronicles:

1 Chronicles: 2:72-75; 3:10-24; 4:1-10, 21-23; 5:4-22; 6:31-53; 8:6-32; 9:1; 12; 15:1-24; 22; 23; 24; 25; 26:29-32; 27; 28; 29:1-25.

2 Chronicles: 11:18-23; 13:4-32; 14:8-14; 15:1-7; 16:7-10; 19; 21:2-4, 12-15; 24:15-22; 26:6-15; 28:9-15; 29:3-36; 30:1-27; 32:27-31; 33:11-15; 34:3-7.

Some of this additional material contains genealogical lists (especially of the Levites), which may not be of particular interest to Latter-day Saint readers, but much of the material will complement their understanding of Genesis, Samuel, and Kings.

One should not read Chronicles as a historical review of

these earlier works. It has its own unique purpose. The writer of the Chronicles (traditionally thought to be Ezra the scribe) presents his genealogies, stories, and facts with a definite purpose. He wants to demonstrate the hand of God in human affairs, especially in the house of Israel. He portrays the moral order and covenant relationship of God with his children. He also stresses the observance of rightful forms of worship for the Israelite community and teaches that God's revelations were given not only in the past but are given in the present as a living word of truth. He reviews Israel's heritage (1 Chr. 1-9), highlights the glorious reigns of David (1 Chr. 10-29) and Solomon (2 Chr. 1-9), and relates Israel's fall from the grace and power of God under her later kings (2 Chr. 10-36).

Read Chronicles as more than history; recognize the moral lesson it attempts to teach, and then it will come to life. (See BD "Chronicles.")

Josiah's Expanded Kingdom
(2 Chr. 34-35)

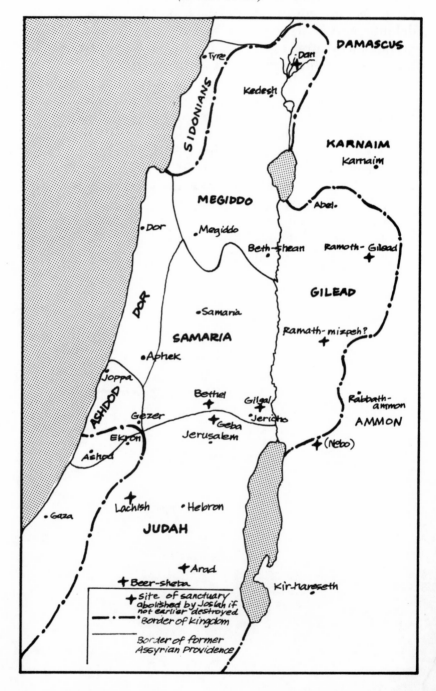

Josiah's Futile Battle
(2 Chr. 35)

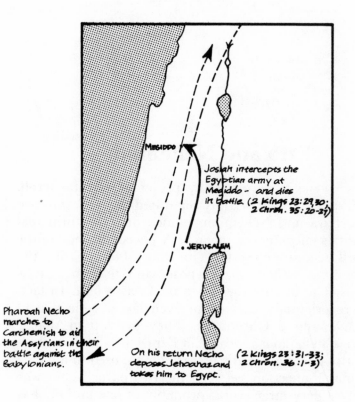

MEGIDDO

Josiah intercepts the Egyptian army at Megiddo – and dies in battle. (2 Kings 23:29,30; 2 Chron. 35:20-24)

• JERUSALEM

Pharoah Necho marches to Carchemish to aid the Assyrians in their battle against the Babylonians.

On his return Necho deposes Jehoahaz and takes him to Egypt.   (2 Kings 23:31-33; 2 Chron. 36:1-3)

Ezra and Nehemiah

These books were originally preserved on one scroll, called Ezra. Early Christianity separated the work into two sections, Ezra and Nehemiah, named after the principal personalities encountered in each. A Jewish division of the work followed much later (in the 1500s). From the standpoint of authorship, purpose, and teachings, it is much easier to discuss these two books as a unit. In fact, they were originally part of an even larger collection of writings, 1 and 2 Chronicles. They overlap in that 2 Chronicles 36:22-23 is repeated in Ezra 1:1-3. Such deliberate repetition was a Semitic literary device used to indicate an original connection between the two parts. What was originally a very large work, probably of one author, has since been divided into four segments: 1 and 2 Chronicles, Ezra, and Nehemiah. Both external factors (the unwieldy use of a large scroll) and internal characteristics (different chronological time periods, events, and personalities) led to this division.

These books are easily organized into four parts:
1. Ezra 1-6: Return of the Babylonian Jews; the rebuilding of the temple.
2. Ezra 7-10: Arrival of Ezra; initial religious reforms.
3. Nehemiah 1-6: Return of more Jews; building the walls of Jerusalem.
4. Nehemiah 7-13: Reordering the religious community.

The writer of these books was probably Ezra (although the work appears to have been modified and edited a few decades later). He continues the theological history of Chronicles (see pp. 110-13) and hopes that the negative experiences of Israel are not to be repeated by his struggling religious community in Jerusalem. If his contemporaries would read his work and heed his lessons, they would be heirs for divine blessings and protection.

The lessons from the past demonstrated that Israel had almost always been in conflict with her political neighbors and the religious environment of the world. The Judean community during the time of Ezra faced similar conflicts as their neighbors opposed them and as they were tempted to intermarry with their neighbors and lose their distinctiveness. Yet if they were righteous, they would be protected from their enemies. The theme of divine assistance was illustrated repeatedly as the author showed how God used different foreign leaders to allow the return and restoration of the Jewish community.

Although contemporary Latter-day Saints are far removed from ancient Jerusalem, the Persians, and the Samaritans, they still face political and social challenges and the pressures of a worldly society. The religious community of Ezra did *not* endure; those Jews fell into a period of apostasy long before Christ's birth. Although Christ's spiritual kingdom of today will remain upon the earth until his second coming, individuals within that kingdom can easily fall away if they disregard the warnings of the ancient scribe, Ezra, and of their contemporary prophets.

Bible Dictionary references: Ezra; Nehemiah; Canon; Cyrus; Gentile; Judea; Scribe; Synagogue; Synagogue, the Great; Temple of Zerubbabel; Temple on Mount Gerizim; Zerubbabel.

Judah after the Return from Babylon
(Nehemiah)

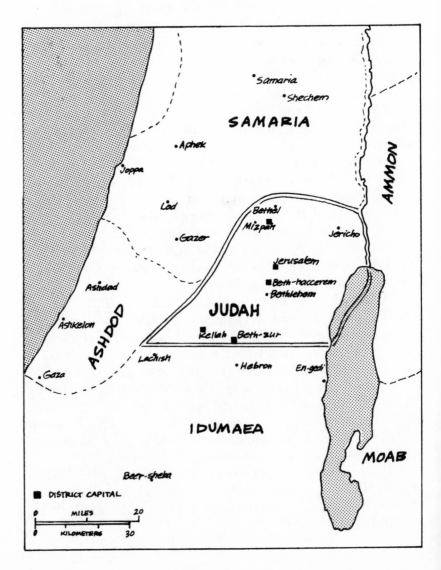

Esther

Esther was one of the last books to be received into the canon of scripture. Various rabbis and Jewish groups before and after the canonizing Council of Jamnia in A.D. 90 rejected the book. It is the only Old Testament book not found among the Dead Sea Scrolls. It is one of two books (along with the Song of Solomon) that does not mention God by name. However, it does show the faith, fasting, and prayers of some Jews in precarious circumstances, and it demonstrates the love the Lord maintains for his children in the house of Israel wherever they may be. (See BD "Esther, Book of.")

The book and the festival of Purim, or "lots," whose origins are described in the book of Esther, continue as an important element in Jewish liturgy. The story is well known to the Jews, and their children love the festival of Purim. Held usually in mid-winter, Purim includes a reading of Esther in the synagogue. The children are dressed in costumes and parade through their Jewish neighborhoods. Then the story is read and acted out. Each girl hopes to be selected to portray Esther. Everyone has noisemakers and they are loudly used whenever the name of Haman is mentioned in the story, in order to drown out any sound of his name. The pageant has the effect of a melodrama. Candy, treats, gifts, and games (usually involving dice or "lots") are an important part of the festival. One can see why it continues to be loved and celebrated by Jewish children throughout the world.

Job

A masterpiece in world literature, the book of Job combines a simple narrative outline (1:1–2:13 and 42:7-17) with classical Hebrew poetry of the highest order (3-37) and the record of a personal revelation (38–42:6) to form a literary work that excites the human senses and a theological treatise that stimulates the divine spirit in man.

Although considered a mythic folk-hero by some critics, Job was a historical personality, as attested to by Ezekiel (14:14), James (5:11), and the Lord (D&C 121:10). He lived for 210 years during the age of the patriarchs (about 2000-1800 B.C.) on the eastern edge of Canaan near the desert (modern Jordan; see areas D-3, 4, 5, Map 1).

Although a righteous, upright, and "perfect" man in his generation (1:1), Job's concept of God's relationship with man was limited. He, along with his friends, assumed that disasters and sorrow only came upon a person because of wickedness. He did not understand that life could be a testing ground for faith and that innocent servants of the Lord could be tried by Satan. He apparently understood the reality of a resurrection, but his lack of remembrance of a pre-earthly spirit existence was compounded with an ignorance of the post-mortal spirit world and how it functioned to provide a complete opportunity for all God's children to receive divine judgments and blessings. In other words, Job was a good, faithful man during a time when the full gospel truths were not available to him.

The book of Job can easily be divided into five parts:
I. The prose prologue (1:1–2:13).
II. Poetic dialogue between Job and his three friends (3:1–31:40).
    A. Job's lament (3).
    B. First cycle of discussion:
        1. Eliphaz (4-5) and Job (6-7).
        2. Bildad (8) and Job (9-10).
        3. Zophar (11) and Job (12-14).
    C. Second cycle:
        1. Eliphaz (15) and Job (16-17).
        2. Bildad (18) and Job (19).
        3. Zophar (20) and Job (21).
    D. Third cycle:
        1. Eliphaz (22) and Job (23-24).
        2. Bildad (25) and Job (26-27:10).
    E. Job teaches about divine wisdom (27:11–28:28).
    F. Job recalls his glorious past and his miserable present (29-30).
    G. Job invites God to be his judge (31).
III. Elihu's tirade (32-37).
IV. The Lord answers from the whirlwind.
    A. The first speech (38-39) and Job's submission (40:1-5).
    B. The second speech (40:6–41:34) and Job's repentance (42:1-6).
V. The prose epilogue (42:7-17).

1. *The prose prologue (1:1–2:13)*. This confrontation between the Lord and Satan over Job has confused Jewish and Christian scholars for centuries. Latter-day Saints should be able to clarify the story by recalling our preearthly existence and the decisions made there. Also, it is helpful to remember that the English word "God" in these

chapters is always translated from the Hebrew word
"Elohim" (a proper name of our Heavenly Father) while
the English word "Lord" comes from the Hebrew word
"Yahweh" (or Jehovah, the premortal name of Jesus
Christ).

Satan was cast out of God's presence long before Job
ever came to this earth. Satan did not return to the celestial
kingdom to question Job's faith, but met the Lord
(Jehovah) somewhere (probably here on the earth) to set
up the conditions to test Job. (Compare D&C 29:39, 47.)
Two rounds of tests followed without Job turning against
the Lord (1:22 and 2:10). Then three sages or friends of Job
came to comfort and help him.

2. *Poetic dialogue between Job and his three friends
(3:1–31:40).* After a week of silence, Job delivers a soliloquy
of his desolation, confusion, suffering, and sorrow. His
friends then rely upon their traditional wisdom to help Job
understand the source of his problems. Eliphaz starts
mildly and reminds Job that he has comforted others in
their times of sorrow. Mortals naturally make mistakes and
need to turn back to the Lord (4, 5). Job responds that his
sorrow is so deep and his life so miserable, yet his friends
are judging him and adding spiritual fears to his physical
torment (6-7).

Bildad speaks more forcibly. He suggests that Job's
family may have been punished because of his children's
wickedness (8:4), his separation from God (8:5-7), or the
sins of his ancestors (8:8); Job should not hide his weaknesses. Job admits the justice of God but contends that
because he is not wicked, God does not condemn him; he
just wants to escape his afflictions and die (9-10).

Zophar chastises Job for his lies and hypocrisy and
exhorts him to repent (11). Job proclaims his innocence
and tells his friends to stop speaking for God, who has true
knowledge of his actions (12-14).

The second cycle of arguments becomes more heated as

Eliphaz outlines the misery of the wicked (15), Bildad highlights the status of the damned (18), and Zophar records the judgments upon the hypocrite (20). Job responds by rebuking his "comforters" who are making life more miserable; he knows he is mortal and subject to death, but he has not been wicked (16-17). He knows that God lives and will judge him as a resurrected being (19). Although the wicked sometimes prosper, God's judgments will come upon them, but he, Job, is innocent (21).

The third cycle breaks down as Eliphaz accuses Job of various sins (22). The second sage, Bildad, speaks very briefly to compare man to a worm (25). The last one, Zophar, does not speak at all. Also, Job becomes more entrenched in his innocence before God (23-24) and he resorts to rebukes (26-27:6) and sarcasm (27:8) to silence his friends.

Then Job turns from the hopeless debate and declares the true understanding and wisdom they all must strive toward. Human wisdom has failed in its ability to understand the mystery of human suffering. His friends have applied the traditional philosophies, while he has argued from the personal conviction of his innocence, admitting that he himself did not know the reason for his suffering. Although they have not solved his problem, they should agree upon some higher principles governing human relationships with God; true "wisdom" is to respect (fear) the Lord and "understanding" is to depart from evil (28:28). In other words, faith and repentance, not material blessings, are the basic principles of a righteous life.

Job recounts his former blessings and good deeds and laments his present afflictions (29-30). He concludes with sixteen pronouncements of innocence and oaths of varied divine judgments to come upon him if he is not telling the truth (31).

3. *Elihu's tirade (32-37)*. A young onlooker, a descendant of Abraham's brother, Nahor (Gen. 22:21), can contain his

frustration no longer and speaks out against Job and his three friends. Although excited and angry, he quotes portions of the earlier dialogue and delivers his own profound, structured insights:

There is a spirit in man that receives divine inspiration (32:8); God speaks to men through various means (dreams, visions, spoken words) while hiding his purposes and a complete understanding of his messages (33:14-17).

No matter how old a person might be, he should appreciate the messenger who helps one understand God's word and repent (33:22-26).

God is just, and man should bear his chastisements (34:12-32).

Men's actions affect others' spirituality (35:6-9).

Man should trust the Lord (35:14).

God is no respecter of persons (36:5-9).

God is great in his knowledge (36:26-32) and power (37).

Elihu's comments do not have the poetic majesty of the earlier dialogue, but they contain sound theological messages that shift attention from Job's question of justice to the divine perspective of the creation. While many scholars feel the Elihu discourse is a later addition to Job, it fits the story well by elevating Job and his friends' attention from his own problems to becoming more receptive to communication from the Lord. Elihu provides the link between the earlier questions and speeches and the divine response.

4. *The Lord's answers (38:1-42:6).* Job finally receives a response from the Lord (Jehovah), although the means (whirlwind) and the approach (a series of questions) were probably unexpected. Job was spiritually sensitive enough to recognize that the Lord was communicating to him. The questions caused Job to ponder whole new dimensions of existence, such as where he was when the earth was created (38:4). That the Lord would even ask Job that question was a divine statement proclaiming that Job was a pre-earthly entity, that he did exist somewhere in some form as the

earth was being organized into its present form. An appreciation of just this one fact must have provided a whole new perspective for Job. The following question and divine utterance demonstrated human ignorance and humbled Job into silence (40:3-5). The Lord's power over the behemoth (hippopotamus) and the leviathan (crocodile) provide simple illustrations of mortal weaknesses when compared to God (40-41). Job finally confesses the rightness of the Lord and his need to repent of any thoughts questioning the justice of God (42:1-6).

5. *The prose epilogue (42:7-17)*. Job and his friends did not have to wait until death or the resurrection to receive God's sentence; their immediate prayers and offerings were required and received. Job became perfect through his suffering. (JD 18:310.) His rewards were not only to be received in the eternities (D&C 121:8, 10), but his possessions, wealth, prestige, and family were all restored to him. He received a double portion of his earlier flocks and herds while his new family was the same size as the old one he had lost (however, with an understanding of sealing powers, his family was now also doubled in size).

In summary, many pertinent and eternal questions are raised in the book of Job, such as:

Why do people suffer?

Why do the wicked sometimes prosper?

Do we do good for a reward or because of our own nature?

Do we appreciate the periods of non-suffering (good health, esteem, ease of life, etc.) which we often have?

What are our answers to the modern philosophies of men (for example, compare 4:17-21; 15:14-16; 25:4-6 with contemporary ideas on the evil nature of man)?

How does one maintain faith in times of suffering or ignorance?

When and how will God vindicate the righteous?

How does God let us know today if we are on the right track?

Can God always be trusted?
Most of these questions are not completely answered in the
book of Job, but by studying the book we should begin to
ponder the possible answers. This process should lead us
toward wisdom and understanding until we are sensitive
enough to receive our own divine responses to these and
other questions. This book not only raises these questions
and gives some answers, but it also challenges us to do the
same. (See BD "Job, Book of.")

The Time Period of Job and the Book of Job

2000 B.C.		1500 B.C.		1000 B.C.
Patriarchs	Bondage	*Moses	Judges	Kings

When Job lived.

When the book of Job
was written in its
present form.

* According to Jewish traditions, the book of Job was first written by Moses in the
wilderness.

Psalms

The book of Psalms is the ancient Israelite hymnal. Unique among the books of the scriptures (which usually contain either God's words to his children or man's writings to man), the psalms record human expressions to God and his Son. In the psalms man praises God (Ps. 9, 24, 30, 33, 56, 67, 71, 95, 96, 150), petitions God for protection and help (Ps. 74, 102, 121), recounts divine acts in human history and among the earlier Israelites (Ps. 60, 78, 104), hopes for the Messiah (Ps. 2, 22, 45, 68, 69, 110, 118), pleads for forgiveness and mercy (Ps. 6, 25, 51), reviews teachings and wisdom of the gospel (Ps. 1, 37, 119), and gives thanks for the divine plan and the roles of the Godhead and men (Ps. 8, 15, 23, 27, 82, 90, 100, 139). After reading just the above-mentioned psalms, only one fourth of the book, one can readily see how poetry, insight, and the spoken word combined to make the psalms great literature and inspired scripture. One can see some of these same themes intertwined in smaller sets of the psalms, such as the Hallal or praise psalms (Ps. 113-118) sung at Passover (even the Last Supper; see Matt. 26:30) and other pilgrim festivals in Jerusalem. Or one can review a small collection of David's psalms, particularly 22-27, to see how he developed many of the same themes.

These major themes and other concepts are scattered throughout the book of Psalms. The book is divided into five sections (1-41, 42-72, 73-89, 90-106, 107-150) each ending with a doxology (short praise hymn). Within each section or the book as a whole, there is no particular order of the psalms by theme, topic, or date of composition (note the similar lack of organization in the current LDS hymnbook), although some psalms are roughly grouped by authorship. However, the psalms of the second and third sections (42-72, 73-89) are mostly addressed to God-Elohim, our Heavenly Father, while the first and last two sections (1-41, 90-106, 107-150) are directed to the Lord Jehovah, our eldest spirit brother.

The book of Psalms is the most popular of the "Writings" (historical and poetical books) in the Old Testament. Almost half of the Old Testament quotations in the New Testament come from Psalms, and Jesus quoted it more than any other book. (See BD "Quotations.") The book of Psalms has inspired countless readers as a classic work in world literature.

To best appreciate this work, study and ponder each psalm individually. Any one of the 150 psalms might be your favorite at this time in your life. As you later reread the book of Psalms, other psalms will inspire and uplift you, and any one of them could provide the special direction or answers you may need.

Bible Dictionary references: Psalms; Fear; Hallelujah; Hosanna; Hymns; Korah; Music; Organ; Selah.

Did David Write All of the Psalms?

No. Some psalms indicate authorship by individuals other than David, such as the sons of Korah (42-49, 84, 85, 87, 88), Asaph (50, 73-83), Ethan (89), and Moses (90). Many of the psalms in the last two sections (90-106, 107-150) have no information of authorship. According to Jewish talmudic tradition, Adam, Melchizedek, and Abraham authored some of the Psalms. (Baba Bathra 14b). In any case, the book of Psalms is a collection of composite authorship that was assembled over centuries of time, down to as late as 200 B.C.

Scholars even question if all the seventy-three psalms with the title "Psalm of David" were written by David. It is not certain that the preposition "of" (in Hebrew *le*) means "composed by." The phrase "psalm of David" could also be translated as "psalm *to* David" (that is, dedicated to David), "psalm *about* David" (written about an event in his life), or even "psalm *like* David" (in the style or pattern of David's psalms). David was noted for his poetry and song writing (see 1 Sam. 16:17-23; 2 Sam. 23:1-5; 1 Chr. 16:4-36) and probably wrote most of the psalms credited to him. (See BD "David.")

Parallelism in Old Testament Poetry and Prophecy

Hebrew poetry comprises about one third of the Old Testament and extends beyond the so-called poetic books (Job, Psalms, Proverbs, etc.); it is especially prominent in the prophetic books (Isaiah, Jeremiah, etc.).

The ancient poets and prophets recognized that their works were usually received and transmitted orally. Although written copies of their works (usually in the form of parchment scrolls) would have been available from generation to generation, most Israelites would not have had copies in their own homes. Temple or synagogue scrolls were usually not readily available, and in times of war or religious persecution they would have been suppressed or destroyed. Rather than relying upon written records, the ancient Semites were trained to memorize long oral passages. The development of their oral retention allowed them to pass on religious records, poetry, psalms, family histories, and other important information.

The ancient poets, prophets, writers, and scribes would assist their followers by organizing their material into a more easily remembered form. Old Testament authors often used key phrases or words as verbal flags to alert the listener to important passages that would be coming up shortly in their presentation. They also used memory devices or patterns that made the poems easier to remember and still allowed the composer spontaneity of expression.

The most common characteristic or pattern in Hebrew poetry was the use of parallelism. Two thousand years after Hebrew had ceased to be a common spoken language, Bishop Robert Lowth rediscovered this memory aid and poetic style in 1753. Later studies have expanded his ideas and have made major strides in understanding Old Testament poetry.

Parallelism is the most significant and distinctive quality of Hebrew poetry. In parallelism, a thought, idea, grammar pattern, or key word of the first line is continued in the second line. There are two basic types of parallelism, grammatical and semantic. Grammatical or "form" parallelism is often difficult to identify, especially in non-Hebrew translations. However, semantic parallelism is more easily recognized in English as it is a "theme rhyme" where the thought or meaning in one line is related to an idea of another line in a variety of parallel patterns:

1. *Synonymous parallelism.* A theme of the first line *repeats* itself in the second line, but in slightly different words:
  (a) A fool's mouth is his ruin, and
  (b) His lips are the snare of his soul. (Prov. 18:7.)

  (a) An ox knows his owner, and
  (b) An ass his master's crib. (Isa. 1:3.)

This most common form of parallelism might be compared to the two rails of a railroad track, because although close together, the repeated ideas reinforce each other and provide a more complete perspective of the major concept.

Many themes, messages, doctrines, and ideas are repeated throughout the scriptures. Repetition is a necessary educational process, whether in learning a new vocabulary word or in understanding complex religious doctrines. By using synonymous parallelism, the ancient authors could repeat their messages and reinforce the learning and memory of their listeners.

2. *Antithetic parallelism.* A thought of the second part of a couplet *contrasts* with an opposite theme in the first.

(a) When pride comes, then comes disgrace:
(b) But with the humble is wisdom. (Prov. 11:2.)

(a) If you are willing and obedient, you will eat the good things of the earth:
(b) But if you refuse and disobey, you will be devoured by the sword. (Isa. 1:19, 20.)

This form is very common in Proverbs, and the use of opposites clarifies both extremes. It might be compared to a black silhouette that brings the exact outline of a figure into sharp focus as it is placed on a white background.

Through antithetic parallelism, the poet mirrors the opposition of all things found in life (see Eccl. 3:1-8). As in life, where sensitivity to ugliness and suffering can lead one to better appreciate beauty and goodness, so also in poetry, the sharp contrast of opposites brings the desired idea or message into sharper focus.

3. *Emblematic parallelism.* The ideas or thoughts of two lines are *compared* by means of a simile or metaphor.

(a) Like clouds and wind without rain
(b) Is the man who boasts of a gift he does not give. (Prov. 25:14.)

(a) Though your sins be as scarlet,
(b) They shall be white as snow.
(a^1) Though they be red as dyed wool,
(b^1) They shall be as fleece. (Isa. 1:18.)

These comparisons are usually recognized by the prepositions "like" or "as." Often, symbolic, emblematic parallelism is like a shadow that can be clear and distinct or hazy and vague.

Symbolic representations allow subtle images and the listener's past experiences to enrich his understanding. Like parables, they allow each listener to comprehend the parallelism according to his or her own background and insights. Thus, every listener can immediately relate to the material and yet still be challenged to develop a new perspective of possible additional meanings.

Note how three types of parallelism are all used in the example above:

red as scarlet	emblematic		
		antithetic	
white as snow	emblematic	(red to white)	synonymous
red as dyed wool	emblematic		(your sins can
		antithetic	be forgiven,
white as fleece	emblematic	(red to white)	your sins can
			be forgiven)

4. *Synthetic parallelism.* The second line *completes* or complements the thought of the first in a variety of possible combinations (question-answer, proposition-conclusion, protasis-apodasis, etc.):

   (a) Yea, though I walk through the valley of the shadow of death, I will fear no evil:
   (b) For thou art with me; thy rod and thy staff they comfort me. (Ps. 23:4.)

   (a) I have nourished and brought up children,
   (b) And they have rebelled against me. (Isa. 1:2.)

The two lines of the couplet are often loosely connected as the second line continues or completes the thought of the first. Like a belt and buckle, synthetic parallelism joins or blends two ideas in any of several possible relations.

Sometimes difficult to identify, synthetic parallelism encompasses good educational psychology, as it generates and answers questions, completes statements, and amplifies ideas. If the first line of a verse seems incomplete or if it causes you to want to know how or why that statement is true (for example, why should I not be afraid in the shadow of death?) that line probably begins a synthetic parallelism.

5. *Composite parallelism.* Three or more phrases *develop* a theme by amplifying a concept or defining a term:

Blessed is the man
(a) Who walks not in the counsel of the ungodly,
(b) Nor stands in the way of sinners,
(c) Nor sits in the seat of the scornful. (Ps. 1:1.)

(a) Ah nation of sin!
(b) A people laden with iniquity!
(c) A brood of evildoers!
(d) Children that are corrupters:
They have forsaken the Lord. (Isa. 1:4.)

By presenting a variety of ideas that radiate about a central theme, this parallelism is often an advanced combination of synonymous and synthetic parallelisms and is like the spokes of a wheel, combining to provide a complete message. Sometimes the central idea (or hub) of these ideas is expressly stated, as in the first example above (qualities of a blessed man). Other times no central theme is mentioned; or a vague general theme or summary might be stated, as with the second example, and the listener must still organize the component parts within a general framework (rim) and complete the model (the wickedness of the society).

Notice in both examples above how the poets provided additional memory or mnemonic aids. In the first, the verb sequence is natural and easy to picture and remember: "walks," "stands," "sits." In the second, the size of the group decreases in each line: "nation," "people," "brood," "children."

Through composite parallelism, the poet expands an idea beyond its simple meaning into its varied component parts. Complex issues are presented in as many facets as the poet wants to develop. He provides the ideas, definitions, and interpretations that give the listeners a more complete understanding of the whole theme.

6. *Climactic parallelism.* Part of one line (a word or phrase) is *repeated* in the second and other lines until a theme is

developed that culminates in a main idea or statement:

   (a) Ascribe to the Lord heavenly beings
   (b) Ascribe to the Lord glory and strength
   (c) Ascribe to the Lord the glory of his name
Worship the Lord in holy array. (Ps. 29:1-2.)

   (a) Your country is desolate
   (b) Your cities are burnt down
   (c) Your land is devoured by strangers before your
       eyes
It is desolate; as overthrown by strangers. (Isa. 1:7.)

The main point and the ideas (or steps) leading toward it can be joined in various combinations. In the first example above, the climax presents a new idea in contrast to the introductory lines. The first three lines stress the majesty of God to the listener, and in the fourth the listener is exhorted to worship God. In this psalm, David develops respect toward the Lord by stressing varied manifestations of divine glory. However, he wants the listeners to do more than just fear the Lord, so he shifts emphasis in the last line and challenges the listeners to worship God in reverence. This poetic style is much more effective than simply saying, "Worship God because he is almighty."

In the second example, the major ideas and key words ("desolate," "strangers") are contained within both the steps and the climax. Thus, the climax is not a surprise but a summary.

Sometimes the theme statement is given first and then followed by the repeated term (a phrase or word) with its attached phrases:

The daughter of Zion is left
   (a) Like a booth in a vineyard
   (b) Like a hut in a cucumber field
   (c) Like a city beleaguered. (Isa. 1:8.)

This progressive model of parallelism is like a set of steps that lead to or descend from a main point. To help distinguish this from composite parallelism, look for a word or phrase to be repeated in each line leading to (or from) the climax.

This complicated form of parallelism is often made by combining a composite form of semantic parallelism with a more obvious example of grammatical parallelism. Grammatical parallelism deals with the structure of the original Hebrew and the syntactic or metrical similarities between lines. Grammatical parallelism is usually present in most semantic parallelisms, but it is often disguised by the English translation. In climactic parallelism, watch for a word, phrase, grammar unit, or other form to repeat itself in each line.

By using a number of close, successive steps, the poet channels the listener's attention toward a culminating point. This climax could be a summary of the earlier mentioned ideas, or it could be a new idea derived from the context of the earlier ones. In any case, the poet uses climactic parallelism to lead the listeners toward a major theme or idea.

7. *Introverted parallelism.* A pattern of words or ideas is stated and then repeated, but in a *reverse* order. This parallelism is also called *chiasmus:*

(a)	*We have escaped* as a bird
(b)	from *the snare* of the fowlers;
(b¹)	*The snare* is broken,
(a¹)	And *we have escaped*! (Ps. 124:7.)

(a)	Ephraim shall not envy
(b)	Judah,
(b¹)	And Judah
(a¹)	shall not harass Ephraim. (Isa. 11:13.)

The poet can develop and then introvert as many ideas as he desires:

| (a) | Make the *heart* of this people fat, |
| (b) | And make their *ears* heavy, |

(c)   And shut their *eyes*.
(c¹)   Lest they see with their *eyes*,
(b¹)   And hear with their *ears*,
(a¹)   And understand with their *heart*,
And convert [return], and be healed [heal themselves].
(Isa. 6:10.)

(abc)   Come to the *house* of the *God of Jacob*, . . . and
             we will walk in his paths
(d)   And he shall judge among the *nations*, . . .
(ef)   And they shall beat their *swords* into *plow-*
             shares,
(e¹f¹)   And their *spears* into *pruninghooks:*
(d¹)   *Nation* shall not lift up sword against *na-*
             tion, . . .
(a¹c¹b¹)   O *house of Jacob*, . . . *let us walk* in the light of
             the *Lord*. (Isa. 2:3-5.)

Chiastic patterns can be expanded to include many verses,
whole chapters, and even (according to some authorities)
groups of chapters. With the more elaborate patterns, a
main theme or message is usually stressed in the center of
the chiasmus; thus it might be compared to an hourglass,
with the focal point being in the middle. The separate
halves of the chiasmus can also be in parallel patterns
(synonymous, antithetic, synthetic, etc.), so this becomes a
very sophisticated style of Hebrew poetry.

Chiastic parallelism is a common literary and public
communications style used by Israelite poets and prophets.
Just as contemporary students in public speaking classes
are taught to organize their talks, ancient Israelite poets
would use chiasmus along with other forms of parallelism
to organize their messages.

Introverted parallelism is found in much of the inspired
prophetic literature, suggesting the possibility that revelation was received by the prophets in this structured form.
Chiasmus (and the other parallelisms included with it)

transmitted sublime, divine teachings, most of which are relevant for God's children today.

Summary: For the people of Old Testament times, parallelism served not only as an oral memory device, but enriched the messages as it provided new dimensions of meaning. Today, an awareness of parallelism aids the reader in his comprehension of vague and repetitive biblical passages.

Why Is Old Testament Poetry So Hard to Understand?

Do not be concerned if you have a hard time understanding Old Testament poetry the first time you read it. Your understanding of the poetry in the Bible (especially in Isaiah) will increase as you read more of the scriptures. Most of Psalms and Proverbs, and Isaiah and other prophetic books are written in the poetic pattern of parallelism, and you will soon recognize the beauty and strength it gives to these writings and the rest of the Old Testament.

Old Testament poetry is hard to recognize and understand for the following reasons:

1. We usually do not know the Hebrew forms of speech, the Israelite cultural settings, or the symbolisms found in the writings.
2. The poet or prophet usually does not explain everything. He leaves much interpretive work to us.
3. When a poetic work is highly structured (such as in chiastic or acrostic patterns) the material is sometimes stilted, stretched, or forced by the author to fit the pattern.
4. Sometimes we want to read into the material more than the author originally tried to present. However, this potential for many, varied interpretations is what gives the scriptures much of their richness and lasting value.
5. We are usually unfamiliar with the parallelistic poetic style, and only as we read and study it can we better recognize and appreciate it.

Musical Instruments and the Term *Selah*
(Ps. 3)

"SELAH"

סֶלָה

Why Are There Hebrew Letters Separating the Different Segments of Psalm 119?

This psalm is in a poetic form known as acrostic. In a Hebrew acrostic poem, each segment begins with successive letters of the alphabet. An example in English would be to have the first verse begin with the letter A, the second verse with B, the third verse with C, and so on. Since Hebrew has twenty-two letters in its alphabet, Hebrew acrostic poetry has twenty-two segments, each beginning with a different letter in alphabetical order. Psalm 119 is the most elaborate form of acrostic poetry in the Bible, with all eight verses in each segment beginning with a particular Hebrew letter. Other psalms (25, 34, 37, 111, 112, 145) and portions of other poetic books (for example, Prov. 31:10-31) are also in acrostic patterns. Since most of Hebrew poetry and psalms were transmitted orally, the use of acrostic patterns would help in the memorization and transmission of this material. Although acrostic poems were sometimes stilted or forced in order to fit the pattern, they provided "memory hooks" that allowed many more people to remember and cherish these inspired writings.

The "Songs of Degrees"
(Ps. 120-134)

These psalms are also called "songs of ascents," meaning songs of "rising" or "going up." These fifteen psalms may have been sung by Israelite pilgrims as they traveled up to Jerusalem for religious festivals. (See BD "Feasts.") In some translations they are called the "pilgrim songs" or the "pilgrim book of devotions." Another possibility is that priests and Levites may have sung these psalms during the festivals as they ascended the steps and courtyards approaching the temple, especially the fifteen steps leading from the women's court to the men's court. In either case, these psalms were part of the liturgy of the Jerusalem temple and ancient Israelite religious holidays. As such, they could be compared with the Easter, Christmas, or Thanksgiving hymns of our age.

Proverbs

This work is a collection of sayings from the wise men of ancient Israel and the Near East. Three sources of instruction were recognized by the Israelites: the prophets (speaking for God), the priests (teaching God's word), and the wise men (understanding God's works). The sayings of these wise men were studied, accepted, and passed on, just as the works of the great writers are today. The wise men did not claim to be giving the absolute word of the Lord, but they were often inspired, and they shared their insights and wisdom in such collections as Proverbs.

Many of the proverbs were written by Solomon. However, he and later kings (particularly Hezekiah) also collected proverbs from the palace academies, other leaders, and the sages in neighboring lands.

The book of Proverbs is organized as follows:

I. The excellence of wisdom (1-9).
   A. Title, purpose, and motto of the book (1:1-7).
   B. Instruction about wisdom (1:8–2:22).
   C. Blessings of wisdom (3).
   D. Wisdom for scholars (4).
   E. Married life (5).
   F. Warnings (6-7).
   G. Praise and value of wisdom (8-9).

II. Collections or sets of proverbs (10-31).
   A. Proverbs of Solomon (10:1–22:16).
   B. Sayings of the wise (22:17–24:24).
   C. Second collection of Solomon's proverbs (25-29).
   D. Words of Agur (30).
   E. Words of Lemuel (31:1-9).
   F. The good wife (31:10-31).

Many individual proverbs are familiar to people who have never read the book in such forms as: "A soft answer turns away anger" (15:1); "A merry heart makes a cheerful disposition" (15:13); "To spare the rod is to spoil the child" (13:24). The book of Proverbs has become not only a part of the scriptures but also a classic work of literature. It shares the timelessness of other famous works.

The classics, be they of literature, art, or music, are loved in each generation because they usually present various contrasts of life and the opposition in relationships such as good-evil, old-young, man-woman, greed-generosity, temporary-eternal, and so on. Proverbs highlights the opposites of: wisdom and foolishness (10:8, 13-14), the righteous and the wicked (10:3, 6-7, 11, 20-21, 24-25, 27-32), the family and society (10:1), work and laziness (10:4-5, 26), speech and gossip (10:18-21, 31-32), rich and poor (10:15), pride and humility (11:2), masters and servants (11:29), hopes and fears (12:25). These sets of opposites are written in a poetic style known as antithetic parallelism (see p. 129). This poetic pattern is especially common in the book of Proverbs. Study it and see how it is used throughout the work. Then study the lessons and ideas being taught and see how they might be applied in your own life. (See BD "Proverbs, Book of.")

Ecclesiastes

Ecclesiastes is an expression of skepticism whose gloomy mood is all the more striking because of its placement between works of optimism (Proverbs) and love (Song of Solomon). It presents the conflict between the philosophies of the world and faith in God. One man, a "son of David" struggles with this eternal conflict.

The "son of David" could be David's literal son, the next king of Jerusalem, Solomon. What man was better able to evaluate life at its best—with spiritual gifts, power, fame, riches, and love—and at its worst—with wickedness, emptiness, a lack of spiritual direction, and a fear of divine judgments. Yet a declaration of faith (Eccl. 12:13, 14) is not recorded in the scriptural accounts on Solomon. Also, the language, style, and some vocabulary come from a later time in Israel's history. It could be a later, rewritten version of a record of Solomon, but more likely it was composed by someone else.

The term "son" in "son of David" in the original classical Hebrew is not restricted to his own immediate family; it means "a male descendant." Terms such as *grandson* or *great-grandson* were not used. Thus, a later descendant of David who himself might have been a king over Jerusalem (as many were for over four centuries) might have composed this work. It could represent either his own struggles, or the conflict of a faithful king in a wicked generation, such as Hezekiah during the time of Isaiah or Josiah during the time of Jeremiah.

Or the term "son of David" might be figurative, meaning "a follower of David." In Ecclesiastes 12:12 the term "son" is used by the author or preacher (as he calls himself in 1:1) as he addresses a listener or disciple. Such a use of the word "son" is seen repeatedly in Proverbs and other biblical literature. Thus, the preacher may be using the life of David as a model to represent the emptiness of physical life without a spiritual purpose. David also experienced the best and the worst of life as he gloried in the praise of God and man before he was disgraced before both. In the depths of misery and sin he repented and he turned back to the Lord. Solomon, however, did not repent and turn back to the Lord, as did David his father. (JST 1 Kgs. 11:33.) Thus, the life of David served as a valid model for the preacher.

The preacher also may have followed his own path of worldliness and attempted to repent. In any case, the question of authorship should not distract from the book's message of how one may struggle and journey toward faith in a world of doubt. He vacillates between faith and skepticism. His weak hopes appear to be stifled by doubt. For most of the book, the outcome remains unsure and faith appears to be defeated, but in the end it triumphs.

The conflict presented in Ecclesiastes could have been that of David, of Solomon, or of a later king or leader in Jerusalem. Almost everyone goes through the same conflict as he struggles to develop faith in a world of doubt. Until one knows for himself, he would be wise to follow the counsel of the preacher and remember that the whole purpose of mortality is to develop faith and to keep the Lord's commandments (12:13). (See BD "Ecclesiastes.")

The Song of Solomon

Rather than a psalm written by or about Solomon (as the title would suggest), this work is a short collection of about two dozen love songs or ballads. According to a notation made by Joseph Smith while working on his translation of the Bible, he did not consider the book to be inspired scripture. It is one of two biblical books (along with Esther) wherein the name of God is not mentioned. Although doctrinally not enlightening, the book can be appreciated through two avenues of study.

One can study the work as a collection of love ballads. The separation of the ballads and the identification of the singers (he, she, or a group of observers) are not clearly marked, especially in the King James Version. However, other translations, including the Revised Standard Version and the Jerusalem Bible, are quite helpful in assisting with this problem. Although quite different from love songs today, these ballads are authentic examples of oriental poetry. They vividly depict the love between a man and a woman. Open and descriptive, but never vulgar, they express the tender, emotional feelings between lovers. Using many images and comparisons, they describe the physical attractions the man and his maiden find in each other. Excitement, anxiety, loneliness, and other emotions are also portrayed by the woman and her lover. With simple innocence, these love poems entice us toward these oriental lovers as we see them through their own eyes and hearts.

A second study of the Song of Solomon could be to consider it as an allegory or representation of God's love for Israel (Jewish interpretation) or for the Church (Christian viewpoint). Latter-day Saints in particular have reasons to identify with this allegory. First, whether the maiden represents Israel or the Church, one should recognize that not every Israelite or Christian can claim this symbolized pure love from God—it is reserved for the covenant Israelite and the member of Christ's true church. Both these titles should apply to Latter-day Saints, and thus they should feel welcomed in the love and embrace of Christ. Secondly, there is one description of the woman in the Song of Solomon that is used repeatedly in the Doctrine and Covenants to identify the restored Church of Jesus Christ.

This description is found at the end of the poem in Song of Solomon 6:10-13. In verse ten, it is asked: *"Who is she* that looketh forth as the morning, fair as the moon, clear as the sun, and terrible as an army with banners?" This is answered in the inspired dedicatory prayer of the Kirtland Temple recorded in Doctrine and Covenants 109:73, where "she" is identified with Christ's restored church, which will "come forth out of the wilderness of darkness, and shine forth fair as the moon, clear as the sun, and terrible as an army with banners." Continuing with the biblical image, Joseph Smith adds that she will be "adorned as a bride for that day" when the Lord would unveil the heavens, transform the earth, and appear in glory. (D&C 109:74.) Further references in the Doctrine and Covenants to the Song of Solomon are sections 5:14 and 105:31, where the maiden is again identified with Christ's restored church and its hosts of members who are sanctified in preparation for the Millennium. (See also "Banners" article in Daniel H. Ludlow, *A Companion to Your Study of the Doctrine and Covenants* [Salt Lake City: Deseret Book Co., 1978], vol. 2, pp. 21-22.)

One other reference to the maiden in Song of Solomon

as the restored Church is found in Revelation 12:1-7. Here John describes a woman appearing in the last days with the sun and the moon. He records that she would deliver her child and prevail over Satan and that she is "the church of God, who had been delivered of her pains, and brought forth the kingdom of our God and his Christ. (JST Rev. 12:7.) Compare Isaiah's description of these events in Isaiah 66:5-13, where he records that suddenly Zion will be delivered by a woman and that she would draw Israel to her breasts.

Although the Song of Solomon appears to be simple love poetry, one can draw from it comparisons to spiritual matters, just as one relates moral and spiritual meaning to other allegories, parables, and stories of the Bible. These love ballads can be appreciated for their own intrinsic and poetic values, and they can also be expanded and applied to the Lord's descriptions of his restored church in the last days. (See BD "Song of Solomon.")

Isaiah

The writings of Isaiah constitute the most important prophetic discourses of the Old Testament. Isaiah is quoted more in the New Testament, the Book of Mormon, the Doctrine and Covenants, and among the Dead Sea Scrolls, than any other Old Testament prophet. Jesus also quoted Isaiah extensively as he began his ministry (compare Isa. 61:1-3 with Luke 4:16-21), taught the Jews, and visited the Nephites. In 3 Nephi, he evaluated the prophecies of Isaiah, proclaimed that all of them would be fulfilled, and commanded his followers to search the words of Isaiah. (3 Ne. 20:11-12; 23:1-3.)

Isaiah was born about 775 B.C. during the reigns of two strong Israelite kings. In the northern kingdom of Israel, Jeroboam II beautified Samaria and expanded his country's borders and influence to their greatest extent since Solomon's time. In the southern kingdom of Judah, Uzziah served as Jerusalem's most powerful king in more than a century. Wealth, social injustices, immorality, and growing pagan worship characterized both societies. This was also a time of peace for both kingdoms, since neither Assyria (to the northeast) nor Egypt (to the southwest) had strong rulers.

Shortly after Isaiah reached adulthood, the two Israelite kingdoms weakened just as one of Assyria's most powerful kings, Tiglath-Pileser III (or Pul, as he was called in the

Bible), came to the throne in 745 B.C. Civil dissensions, rebel rulers, international warfare, and assassinations had disrupted the northern kingdom of Israel, while in Judah, Uzziah had become a leper, a social outcast, and a co-regent king with his son after he tried to burn the priestly incense in the temple in 750 B.C.

Isaiah was called as a prophet about a decade later. In the year that King Uzziah died, about 740 B.C., Isaiah received a great vision concerning his calling (Isa. 6) and was soon recognized by both kingdoms as a prophet of the Lord.

Isaiah says very little about his background, family life, or personal feelings. He had at least two sons, whose names contained prophetic warnings (Isa. 7:3; 8:3). According to Jewish tradition, he was related to the royal family, and one of his daughters married King Hezekiah, the grandson of Uzziah. He suffered a martyr's death at the hands of the wicked King Manasseh, who had Isaiah encased in a tree trunk and sawn asunder with a wooden saw.

Isaiah and his contemporary prophets (Amos, Hosea, and Micah) exhorted the Israelites to return to complete obedience of the laws of Moses. According to his own writings, he did not perform many great miracles although he did promise a miraculous deliverance to Jerusalem (37) and prophesied health to Hezekiah and then gave him a sign or miracle by having the sun's shadow recede (38). His greatest power came not as a lawgiver (like Moses) and not as a miracle worker (like Elijah) but as a prophet and seer who prophesied about many future events in the history of the world.

Isaiah's warnings and prophecies cover almost three thousand years of Israelite history. They also foretell the first and second coming of the Messiah, the restoration of the gospel, the gathering of the house of Israel, the events and leaders before the Millennium, and some characteristics of the Millennium. The following is a brief summary of his writings:

Chapter Description, with major themes italicized

1-12   Warnings to ancient *Israelites and their leaders* with prophecies about later times and leaders (including the Messiah).

13-23   Prophecies concerning the *foreign nations* and their later representations upon the earth until the last days.

24-27   Isaiah's *apocalypse:* prophecies, psalms, and prayers about the judgment of the world and the blessings of Israel in the last days.

28-35   *First judgment, then paradise:* a warning to Israel of her sufferings and to the wicked world (Edom) of its destruction before the Millennium, when the earth will blossom as a rose and the righteous will be blessed with hidden knowledge and scriptures, noble leaders, justice, and peace.

36-39   *Historical narrative* of the Assyrian invasion and King Hezekiah.

40-47   *Affirmation of God's power* and glory with prophecies concerning his servants (both messianic and secular) who will deliver the righteous from death, wickedness, and oppression.

48-52   *Israel, Israel, Israel:* a call to scattered "blood Israel" to join with "covenant Israel" and to become joint-heirs to the "land Israel" and the blessings of righteousness in Zion.

53   The great *servant song of the Messiah.*

54-58   *Encouragements to Israel and the world* to join the Lord's work, to trust in his ways, and to keep his commandments (such as the sabbath, morality, fasting, and charity) and to always turn away from sin.

59-66   Prophecies of *the great and dreadful day of the Lord,* including the gathering, the Restoration, temporal and spiritual blessings, the return of Christ, *and the creation of a new heaven and a new earth.*

It is assumed that Isaiah arranged his writings into their present order, although a scribe or disciple may have done so. Much of the historical material (especially chapters 36-39) is contained in 2 Kings 14-21 and 2 Chronicles 26-33.

Portions of Isaiah's writings (especially his history of Uzziah; see 2 Chr. 26:22) were later lost or corrupted by editing and deletion. Many sacred writings were lost during the fifty-five–year reign of Manasseh, who killed many righteous people and offered his own son as a human sacrifice. The Babylonian invasion and captivity resulted in other lost records. After the return from Babylon, Jewish scribes, led by Ezra, collected sacred writings, compared variant manuscripts, and prepared standardized copies. The accepted Hebrew translation (the Masora) of the Old Testament was a continuation of the Ezra tradition. The contents of the Greek translation (the Septuagint) and the translated biblical portions in the Book of Mormon (which came from the Brass Plates of Laban, taken from Jerusalem before the Babylonian captivity) differed somewhat from the Masoretic text, although the Isaiah material was basically the same in all three versions.

In spite of the passage of time and the ravages and pressures without and within Judaism, most of Isaiah's writings have remained relatively intact. They provide powerful warnings and prophecies to the world from an Old Testament prophet who was great like unto Moses (Deut. 18:15) and who communed with God (2 Ne. 11:2). (See Bd "Isaiah.")

Isaiah's Preface
(Isa. 1-5)
The first five chapters of Isaiah preview his major themes. He denounces the wickedness of Israel and holds

out the promise of forgiveness and eventual restoration in the last days. Most of these concepts are found in the first chapter. Although there are indications that the first chapter and even the first five chapters were written later in Isaiah's ministry, they are deliberately placed at the beginning of Isaiah. The first chapter of Isaiah might be compared to the first section of the Doctrine and Covenants, which was received later than other revelations, but was placed as the inspired preface to the book.

"In That Day"
(Isa. 2:11)

Isaiah almost always uses this phrase to refer to the last days or the dispensation of the fullness of times.

A Woman's Reproach
(Isa. 4:1)

In a Semitic society, the greatest disgrace for a woman was to be barren. Isaiah describes a time when women will support themselves financially, but seek a husband who will make it possible for them to achieve the honor of motherhood.

"Reverse Tithing"
(Isa. 5:10)

In verse ten the seriousness of the desolation in the fields is demonstrated by the terms used. Ordinarily, a farmer would hope to get a thirty-, sixty-, or even a hundred-fold increase from the seed he planted. But instead he would only get one tenth back, because one homer of seed (equal to ten ephahs) would yield only one ephah of harvest. This is a unique type of "reverse tithing."

Why Is Isaiah So Difficult?
(Isa. 6)

Students of the scriptures sometimes sense that Isaiah knew the answers to many important questions concerning the gospel and the last days. They ask urgently, "If Isaiah had the answers to our questions about the last days, why didn't he convey them to us in a simpler and more understandable way?"

Among the answers that could be given are the following:

1. Isaiah deliberately veiled his message so that it would be difficult for the spiritually unenlightened to understand. Indeed, the Lord apparently instructed him to do so. (See Isaiah 6:9-10 and Matt. 13.) Although Isaiah and Jesus faced similar teaching challenges, they used different approaches. Jesus spoke in parables because the Jews at his time saw and heard but often did not perceive or understand. (See Matt. 13:13-17; Luke 8:10; Mark 4:9-13; John 12:37-41.) Jesus went from the simple to the complex, while Isaiah started at the complex level and challenged his listeners to reach up to his level.

2. Because of the drastic contrasts between his age and our own, he undoubtedly found it challenging to describe what he saw. For example, how would he describe modern travel by train or airplane? Can we, today, match his symbols (a great beast, or a bird carrying people off— Isa. 5:26-29; 40:31) with what for us are commom means of contemporary transportation?

3. It is probably good that we do not understand the chronology and details of *all* the events of the last days. Otherwise we might rely on their fulfillment rather than using our free agency to bring about their fulfillment. One major purpose of our earth life is to live by faith and thereby learn for ourselves how we will act toward God and others. Having detailed knowledge of future events and then witnessing the Lord continually fulfilling his prophecies would restrict this purpose and place us in greater accountability to obey the Lord in all things.

4. Isaiah's style of prophesying and his command of the Hebrew language are sophisticated and eloquent. (1 Ne. 25:1, 5; also study "Parallelism in Old Testament Poetry and Prophecy,"pp.127-35. Most of the book of Isaiah is poetry.)
5. Isaiah spoke to scattered Israel and the Gentiles throughout many centuries, not just to the Israelites of his time. (3 Ne. 23:2.) Thus, any one group of people (such as Latter-day Saints) in a particular time might not easily understand how his message would apply directly to them. Many of his prophecies had double or even triple fulfillment in later generations.
6. Ancient Israelites despised words of plainness and sought for things they could not understand. (Jacob 4:14.) Thus, Isaiah spoke without simplicity and plainness. Also, some of his "plain and precious" words may have been edited or deleted by later generations of Jewish scribes.
7. Ancient Israelites were wicked and unworthy to have the truth plainly revealed to them. (Isa. 1:3, 4; 2 Ne. 25:2.)
8. The insights one gains from the scriptures and especially Isaiah depends upon one's spiritual development and worthiness to receive greater light and truth. (2 Ne. 28:30.) Each person should develop his own gift of prophecy and understanding as he reads Isaiah and then ponders and prays.

However, the Lord desires that we understand the timing and fulfillment of some prophecies concerning our dispensation. In keeping with the principles of "line upon line, precept upon precept" (Isa. 28:10; 2 Ne. 28:30), he makes it possible for us to understand more as we are spritually prepared. Nephi said, speaking of the prophecies of Isaiah, "Men shall know of a surety, at the times when they shall come to pass." (2 Ne. 25:7.) This knowledge strengthens our faith in his prophecies, and it challenges us to study his messages so we can be better prepared for the problems of our day.

Because many of Isaiah's prophecies are being fulfilled in these last days, we have a better opportunity to understand his writings than any other generation. We also have other scriptures and living prophets that enlighten us about Isaiah's words. Although Isaiah is difficult, even deliberately difficult, he is not impossible to understand if we will study the scriptures, review contemporary events, listen to the living prophets, and, above all, heed the promptings of the Spirit. His words can become clear to each of us.

Uzziah's Society
(Isa. 6:1)

Throughout King Uzziah's administration, Israel and Judah were wealthy and relatively powerful. Luxury had, however, brought about great social injustices—greed, envy, idleness, and drunkenness. The wealthy took advantage of the poor through heavy taxation. Rejection of the Lord and turning toward pagan gods became common. Religion became a matter of ritual and sacrificial offering. Immorality prevailed. Isaiah's call to the ministry came during the decline of Judah's and Israel's power, prosperity, and spirituality.

Promises for Israel
(Isa. 7-12)

Set in the midst of political problems, chapters 7-12 promise both an immediate military deliverance from Judah and a future redemption and glory for all Israel. The source of both victories will be the Lord—the Lord Jehovah, God of the Old Testament, for immediate protection, and the Lord Jesus Christ, God of the New Covenant, for eternal salvation.

Isaiah refers to the Lord throughout these chapters in varied, disguised references, including his Immanuel prophecy (7:14); the stumbling block prediction (8:14); and the inspired writings about the "everlasting Father, The

Prince of Peace" (9:6), which motivated later great composers. He also foretold the noble justice of the Lord (11:2-4) and his righteousness and faithfulness (11:5).

These chapters also contain the prophecy that most of us think of first when we try to picture the conditions of the Millennium: "The wolf also shall dwell with the lamb," the leopard with the kid, and the calf with the lion. Wild and tame animals and children and poisonous serpents will play together as the earth is covered with peace and knowledge (11:6-9). Also, all Israel will be united and "Ephraim shall not envy Judah, and Judah shall not vex Ephraim" (11:13). The Lord will be among us as we sing praises in that glorious day (12:5-6).

Syria and Israel against Judah
(Isa. 7:1)

During the reign of Ahaz, a major crisis occurred, the Syro-Ephraimite war (c. 734 B.C.). Pekah, king of Israel, and Rezin, king of Syria, threatened to capture Jerusalem and replace Ahaz with a king of their own choosing for the purpose of forming a tripartite alliance consisting of Syria, Israel, and Judah against Assyria. Isaiah revealed the plot to Ahaz and prophesied that such an alliance would fail; the prophet tried in vain to convince Ahaz to place his trust in the Lord rather than in foreign alliances. Instead, Ahaz made an agreement with the Assyrian monarch, Tilgath-pileser III (Pul), and Judah became a vassal state, paying tribute to Assyria to escape the threat of Syria and Israel.

Strange Names for Isaiah's Sons
(Isa. 7:3)

Isaiah had at least two sons, She-ar-ja-shub (7:3) and Ma-her-shal-al-hash-baz (8:3). The meanings of these names were respectively "a remnant shall return" and "the spoil speedeth, the prey hasteth," symbolic, at least in part, of Isaiah's message to his people. *She-ar-ja-shub* symbolizes

the fact that a remnant of Israel will return to Palestine
after their exile; *Ma-her-shal-al-hash-baz* symbolizes the
warning to the northern kingdom, Israel, whose people and
wealth were to be carried away by Assyria.

A note for the curious: the name Mahershalalhashbaz is
the longest word in the King James Version of the Old
Testament.

Gentle Waters versus a Flood
(Isa. 8:6)

As the Israelites rejected the gentle, flowing waters of
Siloam (see Map 17), which represented the soft promptings of the Spirit, the Lord promised them instead the flood
of the mighty Euphrates, which would come up to their
necks. Then they might finally listen to the Lord.

Invasion toward Jerusalem
(Isa. 10:28-32)

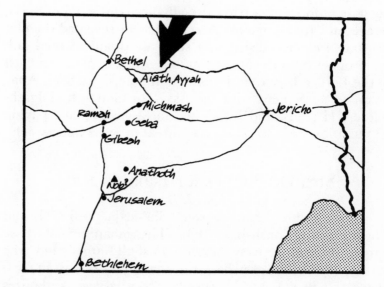

Why Is the Eleventh Chapter of Isaiah So Important to Latter-day Saints?

In sweeping panoramic visions, the Lord taught Isaiah remarkable truths about our time. When Moroni visited Joseph Smith on the night of September 21, 1823, he quoted the eleventh chapter of Isaiah and told Joseph that "it was about to be fulfilled." (JS-H 2:40.) This important chapter describes people and events associated with the Millennium. It contains some classic verses about the wolf and the lamb dwelling together and how Israel will be gathered a second time.

Verse one carries over some of the ideas introduced in the previous chapter where the Lord warns Assyria of her pride and eventual fall. The time would come when the oppressed of Israel would have power over the oppressor. The mighty trees (or leaders) of Assyria would be hewn down (or humbled). Isaiah begins his prophecy in chapter eleven speaking of *new* trees (or leaders) that would come forth out of Israel to rule and bless the earth.

This verse appears to be an example of synonymous parallelism, a poetic device used by Isaiah in nearly every chapter. Apparently in this reference to two separate individuals (rod=branch; stem=roots) he is saying the same thing twice, but in slightly different words:

  a. And there shall come forth a *rod* out of the *stem* of Jesse,

  b. And a *branch* shall grow out of his *roots*.

In Doctrine and Covenants 113 the Lord identifies two key terms used in this verse: the "rod" and "stem of Jesse." The "rod" is "a servant in the hands of Christ, who is partly a descendant of Jesse as well as of Ephraim . . . on whom there is laid much power." (D&C 113:3, 4.) The "stem" is Christ himself. (See D&C 113:1-2.) Therefore, the first part of verse one could be translated: "And there shall come forth a descendant of Jesse and Ephraim who shall be a powerful servant in the hands of Christ . . ."

Continuing the parallelism, the second part of the verse ("and a *branch* shall grow out of his *roots*") could read: ". . . yea, a helper from among his children shall come forth."

The term "branch" in the King James text comes from a Hebrew word that appears in only one other place in the Old Testament—Daniel 11:7. In Daniel's vision of the last days, he mentions a "branch" coming from "roots" ("roots" in Daniel is the same Hebrew word found in Isaiah 11:1). This "branch from the roots" would stand forth in the end of days as a leader against the evil king and army of the north. This wicked king would bring about an "abomination of desolation" in Jerusalem and exalt himself above God, until Michael would lead an army against him. (See Dan. 11:7–12:1.)

Many other scriptures prophesy about the "branch" or leader who will build a temple and fight against the wicked king and stand witness of the Lord's final victory in the last days. He is called by many names and titles, including: "my servant, the branch" (Zech. 3:8-9); "my servant David," a "king" over the Jews (Ezek. 37:21-28); "a righteous Branch and a King" in whose days Judah would be saved (Jer. 23:3-8); "a Branch of righteousness" (Jer. 33:15); "a leader and commander to the people" (Isa. 55:3-4); and "David their king in the latter days" (Hosea 3:4-5).

Modern prophets have also discussed this Jewish leader of the last days. Joseph Smith said, "The throne and kingdom of David is to be taken from him and given to another by the name of David in the last days, raised up out of his lineage." (HC 6:253.) In his dedicatory prayer on the Mount of Olives, Orson Hyde prophesied, "Raise up Jerusalem . . . with David Thy servant, constitute her people a distinct nation and government, with David, even a descendant from the loins of ancient David to be their king." (HC 4:457.)

In summary, the servant ("rod" and "branch") of Isaiah 11:1 appears to describe the great Jewish leader of the last days who will be called David. He will be an instrument of the Lord to fulfill the divine plan of events before the Millennium.

Verses two through five describe some characteristics of this leader. The Spirit of God will rest upon him, and other spiritual gifts will be his. He will be led to reverence the Lord. He will judge righteously through the power of discernment. Like the prophets Joshua (Deut. 34:9) and Samuel (1 Sam. 16:7) and Jesus (John 7:24), he will not depend upon the physical senses of man, but upon the Spirit of God, and will be able to judge in righteousness and equity. (See 1 Cor. 2:10-16.) Indeed, "righteousness shall be the girdle [strength] of his loins, and faithfulness the girdle of his reins [sinews]." Just as a branch and its roots share identifying characteristics, the servant is obviously very much like his master, Christ.

These spiritual powers and promises also belong to Christ (D&C 113:2; 2 Ne. 30:9-11) as he is their giver. He promises to share them with his endowed and faithful disciples. (Alma 20:4; D&C 113:8.) As his servants live righteously and increase their spiritual powers, they become more and more like Christ. These verses therefore achieve a double fulfillment as they describe both Christ and his servants. (Compare Ps. 22, 110.)

Verses six through nine describe the millennial period of peace among animals (wolf and lamb, leopard and goat,

lion and calf) and man and the animals (children and
poisonous serpents). The earth will begin to fill the measure
of her creation as righteousness will prevail and as the
knowledge of the glory of God will fill the world even as the
waters cover the sea. (See also Hab. 2:14.) Enmity between
animals will cease and Satan will be bound as men's righteousness and knowledge increase. (D&C 101:26-34; 2
Ne. 30:16-18.) The gospel will be spread to all nations until
"all the inhabitants of the earth shall embrace it." (DS
3:64-65.)

Another major figure of the last days is introduced in
verse ten: a "root of Jesse, . . . shall stand for an ensign of
the people; to it shall the Gentiles seek." The Lord identifies this "root of Jesse" as "a descendant of Jesse, as well
as of Joseph, unto whom rightly belongs the priesthood,
and the keys of the kingdom, for an ensign, and for the
gathering of my people in the last days." (D&C 113:5-6.)

This servant would hold the priesthood keys that would
serve as an ensign for the Gentiles and result in the gathering of Israel in the last days. This servant is often identified
as the Prophet Joseph Smith.

Although Joseph Smith demonstrated the characteristics of the "root of Jesse," he might not be the only
"root of Jesse" in these last days. Many of the presidents of
the Church have been related to Joseph Smith and all have
held the priesthood and the keys of the kingdom that he
held. The "root of Jesse" could also be that particular
prophet who holds the keys when Christ returns to personally preside over his kingdom. In any case, the "root of
Jesse" is a great leader in the Church of Jesus Christ in this
dispensation.

Verses eleven and twelve elaborate on the gathering of
Israel and the role of an ensign. The first gathering of Israel
took place after the Babylonian captivity; the second
gathering will see remnants return from all directions (as
symbolized by different countries: Assyria = Modern Iraq;
Egypt, Pathros = Egypt; Cush = Ethiopia; Elam = Iran;
Shinar = Iraq; Hamath = Syria) and from various conti-

nents (islands of the sea). The Lord will also set up a church (or ensign) for the nations and the scattered outcasts of Israel.

Verses thirteen and fourteen show that after the dispersed of the Jews (Judah) and the remnants of Israel, including the ten tribes (Ephraim), return, they will work together and prevail over their earlier enemies to the east (Edom, Moab, Ammon = Modern Jordan) and west (Philistines = Gaza Strip). The old hostility between Israel (Ephraim) and Judah will cease as they unite their righteous efforts.

Various interpretations have been rendered for the term "tongue of the Egyptian sea" in verse fifteen. It might be the western arm of the Red Sea (or Gulf of Suez) near the Suez Canal. Another possibility is the delta (or tongue) of the Nile that protrudes into the Mediterranean Sea along Egypt's north coast. The most likely explanation would be the large inland sea created late each spring as the Nile overflows its banks and floods a large part of the valley, like a tongue sticking far inland. Isaiah 19:5-10 describes this event in greater detail. This prophecy has been fulfilled since the building of the Aswan Dam and the destruction of the traditional way of life along the Nile.

The Lord will also divert "the river" (usually understood to be the Euphrates River) into seven streams so travelers can walk across without getting their feet wet. Verse sixteen says that a highway will be prepared for the remnant of Israel coming from Assyria (the land on the other side of the Euphrates). Isaiah 19:23-25 prophesies of a highway all the way from Assyria (through Israel) to Egypt. Other prophecies also describe a great highway for the righteous in the last days. (Isa. 35:8-10; 51:9-11; D&C 133:27.)

Although this highway could be a literal, physical road, it may represent any means of transportation, such as an airway or railroad. The Lord did not create a literal road for ancient Israel, but he did prepare the way for them so they would reach their destination. He will do the same for

Israel in the last days, and they will recognize his hand in their return. (Jer. 16:14-15; 30; 31.)

The eleventh chapter of Isaiah contains some marvelous prophecies of the last days. It enlightens modern Israelites about the roles of two great leaders who will prepare the way for the coming of Christ in power and glory. They may be the two saviors, or messiahs known in Jewish tradition as "Messiah ben David" (a redeemer descended from David) and "Messiah ben Joseph" (a redeemer descended from Joseph).

Isaiah also describes aspects of the gathering and how the Lord will prepare the way for scattered Israel to return. Ephraim and Judah will work together against common foes. They will lead the world to a universal knowledge of the gospel and toward the millennial period of peace and righteousness. Contemporary Israelites need to understand these prophecies so they can be directed and encouraged in their efforts toward establishing this golden age.

Prophecies to the Foreign Nations
(Isa. 13-23)

Isaiah not only prophesies to the house of Israel, but he also gives inspired warnings and promises to other nations. Most of these are found in Isaiah 13-23.

Isaiah first addresses Babylon, the ancient country that had ruled over the Middle East until the Assyrians had displaced her. (See Map 2.) Although Babylon was subject to Assyrian rule during Isaiah's life, it would gradually regain power and independence until the New Babylonian Empire would replace Assyria as the major power in the fertile crescent. (Compare Map 10 and Map 11.) Even during the Assyrian period, Babylon represented the world's best culture, learning, literature, and religion (much as the Greek culture was idolized during the Roman period). Isaiah uses the term "Babylon" to symbolize the world and its wickedness.

Isaiah also speaks to Moab (Jordan) and Syria, to the

east of Israel. These peoples gloried in the downfall of Israel and the humiliation of Judah. They are warned of their impending destruction and promised a later restoration.

Isaiah then addresses the countries west of Israel. Chapter 18 talks of a strange land under the protection of God beyond Africa. As Hyrum Smith indicated in his last general conference address before his martyrdom, this land is America. Chapters 19 and 20 contain special promises to Egypt.

To fully appreciate the context and fulfillment of these chapters, one needs to have a fairly comprehensive understanding of the history of the Middle East over the past three thousand years. Since such a historical perspective is beyond the dimensions of this book, one can at least study the general outline of these nations as Isaiah presents it in these chapters.

Peace in the Middle East
(Isa. 19:24)

As late as the summer of 1977, hardly any expert on the Middle East would have dared predict that Egypt and Israel would complete a peace treaty within two years. Yet a modern, political miracle occurred after the November, 1977, visit of Anwar Sadat to Jerusalem. It culminated on March 26, 1979, when these two countries signed a formal peace treaty.

As of the summer of 1980, hardly any expert on the Middle East would dare predict that Iraq (modern country ruling the ancient area of Assyria), with its Soviet leanings and strong anti-Zionist and anti-Egyptian feelings, will ever sign a peace treaty and open commercial routes with Egypt and Israel. Yet according to Isaiah 19:24, it will happen.

Like a Woman in Travail
(Isa. 21:3)

A woman about to deliver a child is trapped by the last events of the childbirth. There is no turning back, and life and death hang in the balance. Isaiah uses such a graphic event to describe some prophecies shortly to be fulfilled. One may observe and even participate in the events, but they cannot be turned back, and anxiety, fear, and anticipation heighten the suspense of the moment.

Judgment of the World
(Isa. 24-27)

These chapters contain Isaiah's "apocalypse" or revelation in which he uncovers the ultimate destiny of the world and its inhabitants: the earth is transformed (24:19-20, 23); the spirits in prison are remembered (24:21, 27); death is conquered (25:8; 26:19); the wicked are punished (26:11-12; 27:7-8); the righteous are preserved (25:9; 26:8-9; 27:6, 9); and Israel and the righteous are gathered (24:13-15; 27:12-13).

Instruction and Promises from the Lord
(Isa. 28-35)

In these chapters, Isaiah first gives us some keys to acquiring knowledge from the Lord; then he promises Israel that sacred records will come forth to enlighten the righteous and to confuse the worldly (28-29). These chapters contain great insights on how we learn and grow in the gospel.

Isaiah then speaks to both ancient and modern Israel. He first warns the ancient Israelites of their misplaced trust in Egypt. The Egyptian armies would not protect Judah. Indeed, Egypt and all its allies would fall to Assyria (30, 31). Eventually the Jews would be gathered back to their land and restored to peace and plenty (32).

Isaiah's words then shift to the last days and some events surrounding the Second Coming as he delivers pronouncements upon the wicked world (33-34) and his famous "the desert shall blossom as a rose" prophecy with the promise of all righteous Israel being gathered to Zion (35).

What Is the Message and Fulfillment of Isaiah 29, Especially as It Discusses the Special Hidden Records?

Some possible interpretations might be:

1. Isaiah was only talking to the Jews of Jerusalem about the Bible and other records that might come forth in the last days in Judea, such as the Dead Sea Scrolls.
2. Isaiah was talking to the branch of Joseph that would cross the sea. Nephi recognized this and either expounded upon the text by giving additional insights, or restored the text by quoting some parts of Isaiah 29 that were originally in the text but were lost before the King James translation was made.
3. Isaiah was addressing the Jews about their records, but Nephi used this material as a transition point to talk about his own record, the Book of Mormon. In other words, he likened the Isaiah description of Old World records to his New World witness and amplified it to give more details or "inspired interpretation" about the Book of Mormon.
4. Isaiah was talking to us in the last days about any number of records, sacred writings, and scriptures that would sometimes appear miraculously and would almost always confound the wise and confuse the unlearned.

Heavens Rolled Together as a Scroll
(Isa. 34:4)

At least three possible interpretations might explain this phrase:

1. The weather phenomena of the last days (D&C

43:45; 133:69) or the manifestations in the skies (Rev.
6:14; D&C 29:13).

2. The heavens will be sealed after the completion of one
    phase or glory of the earth, or the veil of heaven may
    open up indicating a new age (D&C 77:8; 133:69).

3. The work of the terrestrial world will be completed in
    anticipation of the Millennium and the Second Coming
    (D&C 88:95; 101:23).

King Hezekiah's Jerusalem
(Isa. 36-39)

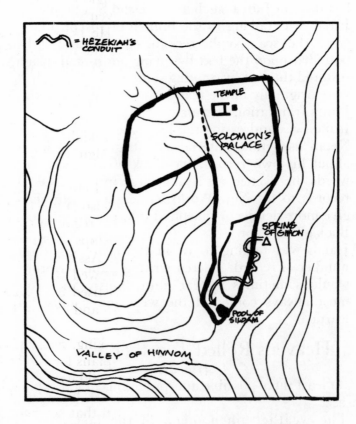

King Hezekiah's Problems
(Isa. 36-39)

Isaiah was not always the best of friends with the king of Judah. Earlier (in chapter 7) he had warned Ahaz to worry less about Syro-Israelite invasion and more about the righteousness of his people. Instead, Ahaz allied with the Assyrians, who quickly conquered Syria and Israel and then deported the ten tribes. The kingdom of Judah was not conquered by the Assyrians, but they were required to pay Assyrian taxes.

After the death of Ahaz in 720, his son Hezekiah became the king. Hezekiah had already ruled together with his father and he had instituted some religious reform. After he became the sole ruler, he became even more zealous in counteracting his father's paganism. He became a close friend to the prophet Isaiah. Although the internal affairs and religious behavior of the kingdom of Judah were improving, the Jews were still subject to Assyrian taxes and armies. Sometime during this period, Hezekiah became gravely ill and feared for his life. After an early warning of immediate death, Isaiah promised Hezekiah fifteen more years of life and gave a miraculous sign to verify this promise (38).

Shortly thereafter, Hezekiah received envoys and gifts from Babylon. The Babylonians were also subjects of the Assyrians at this time, but they hoped to regain their independence and they cultivated the friendships of other rulers who might join in a rebellion against Assyria. Hezekiah tried to impress the Babylonians and showed off the wealth and riches of Judah. He was later chastised by Isaiah for this vanity and was told that the wealth and sons of Judah would be captured by Babylon (39).

Shortly thereafter, a new powerful king, Sennacherib, ascended the Assyrian throne and the plans for a rebellion were halted. Indeed, Sennacherib consolidated his power and ruled with great authority. About 704, he decided that tribute from Judah was not enough and that he wanted to conquer the territory and rule it directly. (2 Kgs. 18:13-36.)

He destroyed some Judean fortified cities and brought his psychological warfare and vast army machine to besiege Jerusalem in 701.

In preparation for this inevitable assault, Hezekiah had strengthened the walls and built a tunnel to bring water within the walls. Hezekiah's tunnel was an ancient engineering wonder, but it and his other efforts were not enough to discourage the mighty Assyrians. In this time of need, he sought counsel and direction from Isaiah, who promised Jerusalem a miraculous deliverance from Sennacherib. After almost two hundred thousand Assyrians were destroyed by an angel of the Lord (perhaps through a plague), Sennacherib withdrew his army and Jerusalem was preserved, as promised by the Lord and Isaiah (36-37). This constituted perhaps the greatest political event in Isaiah's ministry. These chapters also bear witness of Isaiah's authority and the power of his priesthood.

The Lord of this Earth!
(Isa. 40-47)

These eight masterful chapters of Isaiah have inspired Israelites and Christians, composers and theologians, lay persons and ecclesiastical leaders for centuries. The first two chapters were used by Luke in his gospel, by Handel in the *Messiah*, by Brahms in his *Requiem*, and in the well-known hymn "How Firm a Foundation." Each chapter merits hours of study and pondering.

These chapters present different attributes of God, such as: his role as a shepherd (40:11); his omnipotence, omnipresence, and omniscience (40:12-28; 41:1-4); his strength for those who trust in him (40:29-31); his care for Israel (41:8-16); his service to the world (42:1-9); his anger and judgments upon the wicked (42:10-25); his love and blessings for the righteous (43:1-10); his relationship with the house of Israel (43:8-13; 44:1-8); his preparation for the Millennium (43:14-21); his forgiveness of sins (43:22-25; 44:21-28); his names, titles, and roles (scattered throughout these chapters, especially in 44 and 45); and his final acceptance by the world as the only God of this earth (45:5, 6, 14, 21-23). Many other attributes of God are also mentioned in these chapters.

In the chapters 46 and 47, Isaiah turns from his earlier sublime teachings about the Lord and denounces the idol worshippers and those of Israel who do not worship the true God. He uses sarcasm (46:5-7) and sharp words (48:4-8) to impress his message upon his listeners.

Prophetic Past Tense
(Isa. 42:9)

Often when ancient prophets would speak of future events, they would use a verb form sometimes called the "prophetic past tense." That is, they would talk about the future as though the event had already happened. For example, one could talk about the still-future Millennium by saying: "And at the beginning of the Millennium the Church of Jesus Christ had already organized over 10,000 stakes and this number increased ten-fold in ten years. The Latter-day Saints were zealous in sharing the gospel with all people." Study Isaiah 42:9 with D&C 93:24 and see why a prophet would be so confident of the future that he would talk of it in a prophetic past tense.

Speaking to Israel
(Isa. 48-52)

In these few chapters, Isaiah defines the relationship of the Lord to various segments or types of Israelites and tells them how they can find strength in the Lord. He also includes some servant songs and promises about the gathering of Israel. All of these chapters were quoted in the Book of Mormon, especially chapter 52, which was quoted by Jacob (2 Ne. 8:24-25), Abinadi (Mosiah 12:21-24; 15:14-19, 28-30), and Jesus Christ (3 Ne. 20). These chapters helped many ancient Israelites understand their covenants with the Lord and his promises to them. Modern members of covenant Israel continue to find great inspiration in these chapters.

The Waters of Judah
(Isa. 48:1)

This phrase is clarified in the Book of Mormon. The additional phrase "or out of the waters of baptism" in 1 Nephi 20:1 was not in the original 1830 edition of the Book of Mormon. Joseph Smith included it in later editions as an inspired interpretation to help us understand the meaning of the phrase "waters of Judah."

The Servant Songs
(Isa. 49)

Special psalms, poems, or songs about some servants of the Lord are found in Isaiah 42, 49, 50, 52, and 53. Various identifications of these servants have been made. As you read the servant songs, see how any one of the identifications might be the one Isaiah is describing. These possible identities include:

1. Isaiah himself.
2. Israel as a people.
3. Jesus Christ.
4. Joseph Smith (or other latter-day prophets).
5. David, the great leader of the Jews in the last days.

It is perhaps helpful to identify exactly which person Isaiah might be describing, but it is even more enlightening to analyze the characteristics which these servants have and see how they are being developed in our own lives.

A Covenant People
(Isa. 49:8)

Modern Jews are often asked "Why are you the chosen people of God?" They sometimes reply: "It is not just because the Lord has chosen us but because we in each generation continue to choose the Lord as our God." What answer might Latter-day Saints give to this question?

The Great Messiah
(Isa. 53)

The servant song of Isaiah 53 is undoubtedly the most profound of Isaiah's writings. In verses 1-3, Isaiah briefly reviews Jesus' youth and public ministry. He concludes in verses 10-12 with some words about Christ's blessing in the eternities. However, Isaiah presents his most important concepts about Christ's role during mortality in the middle verses (4-9). These key verses highlight the atoning sacrifice of Jesus. Because of the Atonement, we rightfully call him Jesus *Christ* or Jesus the *Messiah*, since these honorary titles are derived from Greek and Hebrew words that refer to his role as our Savior.

Jesus is our Savior because he fulfilled the demands of justice and opened the gates of mercy, which lead to the resurrection and eternal life. Because of his perfect life as the Son of God and his perfect love for us, he bore our griefs (or sicknesses) and carried our sorrows (or sins). (Isa. 53:4.)

The law of justice works in relationship to the other laws of God in the moral realm. In essence, the law of justice might be explained as follows:

1. Every law has both a punishment and a blessing attached to it.
2. Whenever a law is transgressed, a punishment must be inflicted.
3. Whenever a law is kept, a blessing must be given.

The law of justice requires that God must be a God of order and that he must be just and impartial. Because of the law of justice, God can make such statements as these: "I, the Lord, am bound when ye do what I say; but when ye do not what I say, ye have no promise" (D&C 82:10); "There is a law, irrevocably decreed in heaven before the foundations of this world, upon which all blessings are predicated—And when we obtain any blessing from God, it is by obedience to that law which it is predicated." (D&C 130:20-21.)

The law of mercy agrees entirely with the law of justice. However, the law of mercy introduces the possibility of vicarious payment of the penalty for laws that have been transgressed. In essence, the law of mercy might be paraphrased as follows: Whenever a law is transgressed, a payment must be made; however, the person who transgressed the law does not need to make payment *if* he will repent and *if* he can find someone else who is both *able* and *willing* to make payment. The law of mercy insists that the demands of the law of justice be met fully. As Alma stated, "Justice exerciseth all his demands, and also mercy claimeth all which is her own; and thus, none but the truly penitent are saved. What, do ye suppose that mercy can rob justice? I say unto you, Nay; not one whit. If so, God would cease to be God." Alma 42:24-25.)

The law of justice made the atonement of Jesus Christ *necessary*. When Adam fell, he transgressed a law that had physical and spiritual death as its punishment. Thus, the law of justice demanded payment for the broken law.

The law of mercy made the atonement of Jesus Christ *possible*. In order for Jesus Christ to pay fully for the law Adam had transgressed, it was necessary that the Savior be both *able* and *willing* to make atonement. He was *willing* to make payment because of his great love for mankind, and he was *able* to make payment because he lived a sinless life and because he had the power to atone for the spiritual and physical deaths introduced by the fall of Adam and Eve. Because of this atonement, he is rightfully referred to as the Savior *and* Redeemer of all mankind. (See MD pp. 60-66; DS 1:126.)

Every person benefits *unconditionally* from two major aspects of atonement: the resurrection and the full payment for the original transgression of Adam and Eve. However, as Mosiah indicates, there are also some *conditional* aspects of the atonement, and in order to benefit from these a person must repent of his sins. Otherwise, "mercy could have no claim" upon the person, for the law of mercy is made active in the life of a person only upon the conditions of repentance. (Mosiah 3:25-27.)

In summary, Christ fulfilled many demands of the law of justice and brought into effect the powers of the law of mercy. These two laws are diagrammed in the following chart. Note how the law of mercy provides an alternate means of satisfying justice after a person has repented.

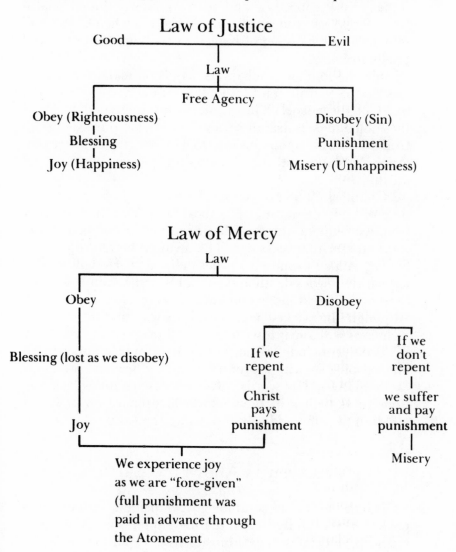

Isaiah's Hopes
(Isa. 54-66)

These last chapters contain Isaiah's messages to the whole world. His words go out to all people as he challenges them concerning their attitudes, relationships with others (especially the needy), and manner of worship. He also holds forth the promise of a millennial era when Christ will return to rule as King of Kings over a world of peace and prosperity.

The discourses in chapters 54-58 of Isaiah contain a promise of Gentiles and Israelites uniting and enjoying the fruits of the gospel. The whole world is invited to share these blessings as Isaiah reviews the divine purpose for all God's children upon this earth. He stresses faith, repentance, Sabbath and temple worship, prayer, charity, and fasting.

Chapters 59-66 are among the most optimistic and sublime of Isaiah's writings. To those who have turned away from wickedness, the Lord has beautiful promises of material and spiritual blessings. The awaited herald of joy, the Savior, is also promised in these chapters. He will release the captives from death and sin in his first coming (61) and become the great judge and king at his second coming (63). Although the wicked will be full of fear at that day, the righteous will await it with hope and prayer.

Isaiah concludes his important book of pronouncements and prophecies with a promise of a new heaven and a new earth (65-66). His words have inspired countless generations of Israelites in their efforts to prepare all of God's children to come and worship before the Lord (66:23).

Heaven Is Above the Earth
(Isa. 55)

Isaiah's ability to combine gospel insights with inspired poetry is beautifully illustrated in chapter 55. Isaiah hints at the premortal and postmortal lives of all people as he reviews how rain and the word of God come from his presence to this earth and then return, having fulfilled their missions—one physical and the other spiritual. He then suggests that we children of God have similar missions to fulfill as part of the Lord's eternal plan (12, 9). The following table outlines Isaiah's poetic style (chiasmus) and highlights his profound teachings:

Verse	*Outline*	*Theme*
1-3	A	Invitation to come to the gospel through baptism; to anyone who seeks eternal life.
4-5	B	Leader and help promised to Israel.
6-7	C	Return to the Lord (repent) and seek his mercy.
8	D	God's thoughts (plans) are not your thoughts (plans).
9	E	The heavens are higher than the earth (divine plans are better than mortal proposals).
13	A^1	The Millennium; we who return to God will be an everlasting sign that God's plan works.
12	B^1	We will be led home (heaven).
10-11	C^1	Rain and God's word return to heaven, their tasks completed.
9	D^1	God's thoughts are above your thoughts.

Isaiah's message: We come to the earth and return (repent) so we can fulfill God's plan of immortality and eternal life and then serve as an everlasting witness of God and his plan, which is high above the plans of men and Satan.

Why Do We Not Always Feel Close to Our Heavenly Father?
(Isa. 59:1)

Sometimes God will leave his children alone in times of trial or sorrow (such as Jesus on the cross or Joseph Smith in Liberty Jail), but usually if we are separated from God, it is because of our own actions. Read Isaiah 59 to find some transgressions that could create a barrier between the Lord and us.

What Is a Cockatrice?
(Isa. 59:5)

Look up the term in the LDS Bible Dictionary (p. 647) and study verses five and six. Cockatrice eggs and spiderwebs might be compared with the devil (the serpent) and the bonds of sin. Isaiah is describing how people give themselves over to Satan's power.

Why Would Our Sons Marry Us?
(Isa. 62:5)

Joseph Smith in his inspired translation changed the word "sons" to "God." This not only clarifies the phrase but it also makes a better synonomous parallelism between the four parts of the verse so that they now compare as follows:

    (a) As a man marries a virgin,
    (b) So does God marry [make a covenant] with us;
    (a¹) As the groom rejoices over his bride,
    (b¹) So does God rejoice over us.

Who Is Talking to Whom in This Chapter?
(Isa. 63)

Isaiah 63 is a dialogue between Isaiah and the Messiah, but there are no quotation marks to separate the speakers. See if you can identify Isaiah's question and the Lord's response in verse one, and then Isaiah's second question in verse two and the Lord's answer in verses 3-6. Verses 7-19 are Isaiah's response. The importance of this chapter will become more clear after studying the following Bible footnotes: 2b and 3c, 3b and 4b, 9b and 9c (including D&C 133:53 and Abr. 1:15), 14d, 16a, and 17a.

Why Would Christ Come from Edom in the Last Days?
(Isa. 63:1)

By using some of the Bible aids, we can find two good

possible answers. First, look at Map 7 or 9 and find Edom or Bozrah in the area southeast of the Salt (or Dead) Sea. Anyone coming from this area to Jerusalem would usually travel north along the King's Highway through Moab and then swing west to cross the Jordan Valley and climb up the mountains.

Secondly, review footnote 1b and see how the term "Edom" (later called "Idumea") symbolically represents the "world" as revealed in Doctrine and Covenants section one.

Thus Isaiah's describing the second coming of Christ as being from Edom could have two meanings:
1. From the east (a direction).
2. From the wicked world (a condition).

The next verses in Isaiah 63 describe how Christ's robes have been soiled as he has come from the wicked world and has cleansed it.

Why Does Isaiah Usually Mix Bad and Good News Together in a Chapter?
(Isa. 66)

Isaiah often begins a chapter in a negative tone as he rebukes sinners and their wickedness. He then holds out a promise of blessings and restoration as the people repent. But he does not end on a high, optimistic note; instead he usually concludes with a sober admonition or warning. This pattern could be diagrammed as follows:

See if you can identify this pattern in Isaiah 66.

This pattern is also found in the collection of all sixty-six chapters of Isaiah. Chapter 66 summarizes the book of Isaiah and provides a last promise and warning to Israel.

Jeremiah

The book of Jeremiah is important for many reasons. First, it is one of the largest books in the scriptures (second only to Psalms). Second, it contains many warnings and prophecies for the House of Israel, especially the Jews. Third, it presents the personality and burdens of a prophet in greater depth than any other book.

The contents of the book include prose and poetry, history and biography, warnings and prophecies. The book has three sets of records and an appendix:

1. Prophecies against Judah and Jerusalem (1-24).
2. Jeremiah's biography and further prophecies, especially of the last days (25-45).
3. Prophecies to the foreign nations (46-51).
4. Historical appendix (52).

The material in the first two dozen chapters is organized in probable chronological order, as these prophecies and warnings were delivered during the reigns of the three major kings, Josiah, Jehoiakim, and Zedekiah. (See BD "Jeremiah"; "Josiah.") Chapters 25-45 are also roughly chronological, but they overlap the earlier chapters (25-27 revert to the time of Jehoiakim and 27:12 to 29:32 are again during Zedekiah's reign). More importantly, they include prophecies of the last days and many biographical insights into the life and struggles of Jeremiah. The next set of prophecies (46-51) deal with various foreign nations. They were originally given at different, scattered times through-

out Jeremiah's ministry and later arranged into their present order. The last chapter contains much of the historical
material found in 2 Kings 24–25 and serves as a historical
conclusion to the book.

It appears that the first set of chapters (1-24) was
probably prepared by Jeremiah and written by his scribe,
Baruch. It includes Jeremiah's insights and feelings about
his calling as a prophet. These expressions open up his
personality by showing his love for the people (8:18-22), his
sorrow for their condition (9:1; 13:17; 14:17), and his plead-
ings on their behalf with the Lord (14:7-9). By reading the
following selections, one can begin to appreciate his attitudes about his call and his feelings for the burden he
carried as the Lord's spokesman to a wicked generation:

1:4-10   His calling and initial hesitancy.
5:14   His words would condemn the people.
8:18-22   His love for Israel.
9:1   His tears shed for Israel.
10:19-24   His rejection by society and petition for divine
            counsel.
11:18-20   His petitions for judgment upon those who
            threatened his life.
12:1-4   His expression of personal righteousness (com-
            pare Job 31) and the Lord's response (12:5-6).
15:10-18   His personal frustrations (compare Elijah in 1
            Kgs. 19:4) and the Lord's response (15:19-21).
16:1-9   His lack of a (second?) wife and family; he was
            not to mourn during the destruction.
17:9-10   His self-judgment.
17:14-18   His request for vindication from the Lord.
18:18-23   His life threatened by a conspiracy.
20:7-18   His burdens as a prophet.
23:28-32   His conflict with false prophets.

By understanding the feelings and problems of this
great prophet, one can study the lives and writings of his
contemporaries and see why Habakkuk questioned the
Lord about justice (Hab. 1), why Urijah lost his life for
giving the same prophecies as Jeremiah (Jer. 26), why

Zephaniah called for a great day of judgment from the Lord (Zeph. 1), and why Lehi feared for his life and took his family out of wicked Judah (1 Ne. 1).

Jeremiah is an Old Testament prophet of particular interest to Mormons because he lived and preached in Jerusalem during the same time period as Lehi, the founder of the primary Book of Mormon colony in the Americas. Both prophets had a clear understanding of the destruction awaiting Jerusalem and, since they actively preached this destruction, they were threatened and persecuted.

Both men also received insights into future events concerning the Israelites, and, in particular, they prophesied about a later gathering when the Israelites would return to their promised land and be recognized as the Lord's chosen people. Both prophets anticipated a partial return of Israelites or Jews after the Babylonian captivity and foresaw a later and more significant return when the Messiah would come in power as Israel's great deliverer.

Most Mormons are aware of Lehi's preachings concerning Israel and the last days, but they are usually unfamiliar with the insights Jeremiah had in these matters.

Of special interest to Mormons is the fact that some of Jeremiah's prophecies have been accomplished, although the Jews have not yet recognized their fulfillment. Mormons should also better appreciate how the Lord has prepared the world and the Jews for the manifestation of these prophecies, how they themselves can recognize some prophecies now being fulfilled, and how they can be aware of future events concerning the gathering of the Jews.

Jeremiah was apparently a young man (1:6) when he received his prophetic calling about 627 B.C. (1:2). As he preached to the remnants of the Israelite tribes then living in the Judean countryside, he spoke mainly to members of the tribe of Judah. He was a Levite, but his priestly family lived in the tribal area of Benjamin, and both these tribes had many people living near Jerusalem. Although the northern ten tribes had been "lost" for almost one hundred years, descendants from most, if not all, of the other tribes of Israel were also scattered among the inhabitants. Since the tribe of Judah was so numerous, and because it supplied the kings and the leadership for the whole area, the combined group of Israelites became known as Jews. In fact, the first scriptural reference by a prophet of the term "Jew" is in the book of Jeremiah (34:9).

These Jews were soon to face strong threats to their existence as a kingdom and as a people when the Babylonians sought to control their country. At first, the Jews did not feel threatened by the Babylonians, since peace and plenty had been prophesied by generations of false prophets. In fact, after the days of Isaiah and the righteous King Hezekiah, the Jews had entered into a state of complete apostasy. Hezekiah's son, Manasseh, ruled for over fifty years and not only encouraged this religious retrogression, but offered one of his sons as a human sacrifice. Manasseh's grandson, Josiah, became king at the age of eight, after his father was murdered because of his wickedness. Twelve years later, Josiah began some religious reforms by cleansing Judah and Jerusalem of their idols. He even had the bones of the priests of Baal burned upon their altars.

It was during this religious reform and in the thirteenth year of the reign of Josiah that Jeremiah received his call. Five years later, while the temple was being repaired, a copy of the Torah (the Law) was found among some rubble. After it was read to Josiah, he was so shocked by the extent of the apostasy among the Jews that he immediately ordered all idols in the land to be destroyed and instigated more rigorous religious reforms. The temple was purified and the Passover celebration was reinstated. (2 Kgs. 22-23; 2 Chr. 34-35.) The royal reforms remained external, however, as the people were not converted from their false practices. When Josiah died, nineteen years after he began his reforms, the Jews quickly reverted to idol worship. (2 Kgs. 23:31-37; 2 Chr. 36:1-21.)

Jeremiah then recorded many prophecies about Israel's later return and restoration in the land. The second portion of his writings (25-45) also included some important prophecies about the Jews in the last days.

Jeremiah is a major prophet because of his many writings. His writings are also interesting because of the personal insights they provide, but he is important for yet another reason. In the New Testament, Jesus was asked if he were another Jeremiah. (Matt. 16:14.) There are many comparisons between these two great servants of our Heavenly Father. They both foretold the end of a Jewish state (587 B.C. and A.D. 70) and the destruction of Jerusalem and her temple. In both cases the doom of the city was followed by a dispersion of the Jews. Both were charged with blasphemy because they criticized the formalized religion and the corrupted temple ritual of their times. They both questioned the external sacrifices when internally the people were wicked. They were both ridiculed by the leaders of society and often ignored by the masses. They were both falsely accused and imprisoned. And (if the traditions about Jeremiah's death are true), they both sealed their witnesses with their own lives.

Jeremiah is an important prophet because of his writings and his life. His writings record why Judah fell and how it will be restored. His life shows the heart of a prophet and the model of a true servant of the Lord.

Who Are the Fishers and Hunters among the Israelites?
(Jer. 16:16-19)

In chapter sixteen of Jeremiah, after the Lord states the identification by which he is to be recognized by the Jews in the last days, he says that he will send fishers and hunters among the Israelites (16:16). Latter-day Saints would recognize these individuals as being missionaries of the restored gospel. The results of these missionary activities were mentioned in chapter three of Jeremiah as the Lord told Israel: "Return, O backsliding children, saith the Lord; for I am married unto you, and I will take you one of

a city, and two of a family, and I will bring you to Zion. . . .
In those days the house of Judah shall walk with the house
of Israel, and they shall come together out of the land of the
north to the land that I have given for an inheritance unto
your fathers" (3:14, 18).

Latter-day Saints have not yet developed these missionary activities among all the Jews. Jeremiah suggests that
they will not take place until after the Lord's judgments
have come upon the wicked children of Israel. The reasons
for these punishments are given in Jeremiah 16:17-18. Such
judgments in earlier Jewish history caused many Jews to
repent and turn away from their heathen idols. Later generations of Jews sometimes forgot the consequences of sin,
and this fact perhaps explains *some* of the persecutions they
have suffered in their history.

After presenting the reasons for the Lord's judgments
upon his children, Jeremiah gives a messianic vision of the
Great Deliverer as portrayed in verse nineteen. His authority will be recognized worldwide as the nations (or
gentiles, as translated in the King James Version of the
Bible) of the earth would come unto him saying that their
"fathers have inherited lies, vanity, and things wherein
there is no profit" (16:19). Then, finally, the people would
recognize the hand and power of the Lord, and know that
his name is Jehovah. The fishers and hunters (missionaries)
would help in this conversion process.

Jeremiah's Prophecies on the Gathering of the Jews in the Last Days
(Jer. 16, 23, 30-33.)

Starting in verse fourteen of chapter sixteen, Jeremiah
makes some prophecies concerning Israel's return in the
last days. This return, he says, will be so impressive that
the Israelites will recognize the hand of the Lord in it. They
will refer to the miracle of the return as a means of identifying or recognizing their God—they will no longer know
him as the Lord that brought them out of Egypt, but as the

Lord who brought them from the land of the north and from all the countries where he had driven them.

Latter-day Saints who are students of Israeli history know that the Jews have been gathered home from the lands of the north and over ninety countries of the earth. These Jews, who automatically and immediately are accepted as Israeli citizens under the "law of the return," have returned from countries as far apart as New Zealand and Lithuania, Argentina and India, Canada and South Africa. Most of them have come from middle eastern or eastern European countries to the country of Israel. Shortly after Israel became independent in 1948, one hundred twenty thousand Jews immigrated from Rumania. Over one hundred thousand Jews left Russia, Poland, and Iraq to go to Israel. Over thirty thousand Jews moved to Israel from Czechoslovakia, Hungary, Bulgaria, Turkey, Syria, and Iran. (Martin Gilbert, *Jewish History Atlas*, pp. 97-99.)

As Jeremiah prophesied, many Jews have returned from the north and from the countries where they had been driven. They now dwell in their own land in the state of Israel. However, most Jews living in Israel do *not* identify the Lord as the causative factor behind their gathering. These Israelis would maintain that their country came into existence through political, military, social, and monetary means, not through any divine guidance. This appears to be a contradiction of Jeremiah's prophecy, as he stated that the Israelites would identify their Lord as the force behind their return.

This same type of apparent contradiction is present in many Book of Mormon prophecies concerning the specific gathering of the Jews to the Holy Land. The prophecies state that *after* the Jews begin to believe in Christ, then they will be gathered in from their long dispersion. Obviously, the Jews in Israel do not believe in Jesus as the Christ or as their Messiah.

If the Jews now gathered together in Israel do not recognize the Lord's hand in their return and if they do not believe in Christ, are they, then, fulfilling these prophecies of Jeremiah, Jacob, Nephi, and Mormon? The answer is probably not. However, they are fulfilling some of the lesser-known prophecies of Jeremiah and Book of Mormon prophets; the more famous prophecies mentioned above are yet to be fulfilled by a righteous group of returning Jews.

As Jeremiah prophesied concerning the gathering of Judah, he understood that a key element of this restoration was the attitude of the Jews to their Lord, Jehovah. The relationship between the gathering of the Jews and their attitudes toward Jehovah is presented in Jeremiah 23:3-8; 30:3-11, 21, 24; 31:1; 32:37-40; and 33:7, 8, 10-11, 14-16.

In chapter twenty-three of Jeremiah, the Lord first denounces the pastors, shepherds, or rulers under whose leadership the people had abandoned righteousness and incurred the exile. In verse three, he promises that he will gather his flock out of the countries and bring them back and make them fruitful. The Lord will then set up shepherds over them so that they will no longer fear men but will have trust in the Lord. A righteous Davidic king is promised them. (See Isa. 11; D&C 113; Zech. 3:8; 6:12; Ezek. 34:23-25; Hosea 3:5.) The Lord then mentions again the new identity he will have for the Israelites in the last days (23:8).

In chapter thirty, the Lord promises the return of Israel and Judah. He mentions a period of such fear and anguish that the gestures displayed by men would be comparable to those of a woman in childbirth. This period of time, ushering in the final deliverance, would be great in suffering and distress, but would free the Israelites from their yokes as they would serve the Lord their God and David, their king, whom he would raise up unto them (30:5-9). The Lord promises that he will save Israel, but his divine justice demands that Israel's sins will not go unpunished. Therefore, he will correct Israel "in measure" before Israel can be pardoned (30:11). Later in the chapter, the land and its prosperity is promised to Jacob's children. They will establish their congregation before the Lord, and he will punish their oppressors. Their righteous prince will be close to the Lord, and the Lord will accept them as his people. These events are to take place in the end of days or, in other words, during our dispensation (30:18-24).

Chapter thirty-one contains prophecies about the restoration of the northern kingdom. The promise of restoration as given to Jerusalem is found in chapter thirty-two (see especially verses 36-44).

Chapter thirty-three is a good summary of the prophecies of the last days because it repeats many of the prophecies given earlier in Jeremiah. For example, the Jews and Israelites will return and be cleansed from their iniquities (33:7-9). The people will give thanks to their Lord, and he will bring forth a righteous leader for them (33:10-16). The Lord will remember his covenant with Israel. Davidic kings and Levites will continue to live and rule among the people as assuredly as day follows night. The Lord will not forget the promises he made to Abraham, Jacob, and David (3:17-24).

These prophecies of Jeremiah are open to us if only we will study them. However, they are basically an outline of the events of the last days. Further information about them is contained in the Book of Mormon. (See 1 Ne. 19:15-16; 2 Ne. 6:11; 10:7; Morm. 5:14.)

When one quickly reads Jeremiah and the Book of Mormon prophets and then recalls their prophecies concerning the gathering of Israel in the last days, he remembers that when Israel accepts the Lord (or recognizes Christ as their Messiah) they will be gathered in. This general understanding is basically correct as one surveys the prophecies concerning the whole house of Israel and their gathering.

However, a more precise study of the scriptures reveals that some rather specific correlations can be established between the relationship of the Israelites to their Lord and the gathering back to their land. This is particularly true for one branch of the Israelites—the Jews. One of three conditions mentioned in the Book of Mormon scriptures listed above must precede any gathering of the Jews: (1) that they no longer rebuke Christ; (2) that they come to a knowledge of Christ; (3) that they begin to believe in Christ as their Messiah.

Although any of these conditions could precede a *gathering* of the Jews, the Lord will not accept the inhabitants of Israel as his people until they believe in him as their God. When they are righteous and God-fearing, he will *restore* them to the lands of their inheritance and protect them from their enemies. In other words, although the Lord might lead the Jews back to their land under various conditions, he will not recognize them as legitimate heirs of the land until they properly worship him. Jeremiah recognized this clearly (32:37-41). The Book of Mormon provides more insight into these relationships; it indicates that some Jews will come to a knowledge and belief of their Messiah *before* they are gathered, while others will come to this knowledge and belief *after* they are gathered to their land. (Compare 2 Ne. 10:7 with 3 Ne. 20:13.)

Understanding this fact helps answer two questions that Latter-day Saints have as they attempt to understand the events of the last days: (1) Why are most Jews, who are returning to Israel, nonreligious Israelites who do not recognize the Lord or his hand in their gathering? and (2) Why will great punishments come upon the Jews in the great and dreadful day of the Lord if they are his chosen people? The truth is that nonreligious, nonbelieving, and even "wicked" Jews are today fulfilling prophecies. As they reject the Lord and his laws, he will justly punish them in the future. Knowing this, we can better appreciate the fulfillment of some of Jeremiah's prophecies.

Lamentations

These five hymns of sorrow express the feelings of Judah when Jerusalem and the temple were destroyed by the Babylonians in 587 B.C. (See BD "Lamentations.") They continue as a part of Jewish liturgy and are recited late each summer in remembrance of the destruction of the temples of Solomon and Herod, which occurred on the same day (ninth of Ab) six hundred fifty-seven years apart. Lamentations 4:1-13 is quoted below in a modern translation prepared by the Jewish Publication Society. Compare this with the King James Version and try to appreciate the genuine remorse being expressed.

1 Alas!
    The gold is dulled,
    Debased the finest gold!
    The sacred gems are spilled
    At every street corner.
2 The precious children of Zion;
    Once valued as gold—
    Alas, they accounted as earthen pots,
    Work of a potter's hands!
3 Even jackal offer the breast
    And suckle their young;
    But my poor people has turned cruel,
    Like ostriches of the desert.
4 The tongue of the suckling cleaves
    To its palate for thirst.

Little children beg for bread;
None gives them a morsel.
5 Those who feasted on dainties
Lie famished in the streets;
Those who were reared in purple
Have embraced refuse heaps.
6 The guilt of my poor people
Exceeded the iniquity of Sodom,
Which was overthrown in a moment,
Without a hand striking it.
7 Her elect were purer than snow,
Whiter than milk;
Their limbs were ruddier than coral,
Their bodies were like sapphire.
8 Now their faces are blacker than soot,
They are not recognized in the streets;
Their skin has shriveled on their bones,
It has become dry as wood.
9 Better off were the slain of the sword
Than those slain by famine,
Who pined away, [as though] wounded,
For lack of the fruits of the field.
10 With their own hands, tender-hearted
    women
Have cooked their children;
Such became their fare,
In the disaster of my poor people.
11 The Lord vented all His fury,
Poured out His blazing wrath;
He kindled a fire in Zion
Which consumed its foundations.
12 The kings of the earth did not believe,
Nor any of the inhabitants of the world,
That foe or adversary could enter
The gates of Jerusalem.
13 It was for the sins of her prophets,
The iniquities of her priests,
Who had shed in her midst
The blood of the just.

Why Did the Israelites Raise Their Hands in Prayer?

(Lam. 3:41)

Many scriptures suggest the raising of one's spirit, soul, voice, or heart toward God (for example 2 Kgs. 19:4; Ps. 25:1; 143:8; Enos 4; D&C 25:13; 27:15; 30:6; 31:3; 35:26). The Israelites also included the physical act of raising their hands as they prayed.

David compared the incense and sacrifices of the tabernacle-temple with his own prayers and the lifting up of his hands (Ps. 141:2). These actions were all brought before the Lord and were raised up toward him. The raising of one's arms was similar to the ascending incense.

Solomon raised his hands as he dedicated the temple (1 Kgs. 8:22). Isaiah wrote that the Israelites stretched forth their hands in unanswered prayers (Isa. 1:15). Enoch, when he had stretched forth his arms in prayer, received an answer from the Lord (Moses 7:41).

Additional associations with the raising of hands in prayer is explained by Hugh Nibley:

> What H. Leclercq calls "that magnificent gesture" of raising both hands high above the head with which those in the prayer circle began their prayer was, as he notes, a natural gesture both of supplication and submission. It was specifically a conscious imitation of the crucifixion, and that brings to mind the significant detail, mentioned by the Synoptic writers, that the Lord on the Cross called upon the Father in a strange tongue: those who were standing by, though Aramaic was supposed to be their native tongue, disagreed as to the meaning (see Mark 15:33ff.), and indeed the Mss give many variant readings of an utterance which the writers of the Gospels left untranslated, plainly because there was some doubt as to the meaning. It recalls the cry of distress of David in Psalm 54:2: "Hear my prayer, O God; give ear to the words of my mouth," and in Psalm 55:1: "Give ear to my prayer, O God. . . . (Hugh Nibley, "The Early Christian Prayer Circle," *Brigham Young University Studies*, Fall, 1978, p. 53.)

Modern Orthodox Jews still use their hands as they pray. They usually do not pray with folded arms, especially when they are praying out loud. If not holding a prayer book in their hands, they often have their hands in front of them while moving and even raising them.

Ezekiel

Raised in Judah, Ezekiel was taken with ten thousand other Jews to Babylon in 597 B.C. Four years later, when he apparently was thirty years old, he received his first vision (1:1). As he recorded this vision, he described God's throne and the cherubim attending it in great detail, but the reader is still puzzled as to how to picture what he saw.

He received five specific charges from the Lord:

1. He was to warn Israel, who would be hostile and stubborn (2:1-8).

2. He was to speak only to Israel; even though they would ignore him, he would be fortified with a "stone forehead" (like a "tough skin" today; 3:7-9).

3. He was to receive, understand, and proclaim to the exiles all that the Lord told him (3:10-15).

4. He was to be a watchman to Israel (3:16-21; compare 33:1-20).

5. He was to return home and be dumb (not speak) until he received word of Jerusalem's destruction (which occurred seven and one half years later; 3:22-27; compare 24:27; 33:22).

The fifth charge or commission is particularly puzzling. It is unclear whether his silence was to be only outside the house, or if he was only to speak the oracles and prophecies given him by the Lord and nothing else, or if he was to be completely silent for the whole time.

Perhaps because of his dumbness, he performed a number of symbolic acts that served as vivid teaching demonstrations about the impending destruction upon Jerusalem:

1. He drew a sketch and used an iron plate to portray siege (4:1-3).
2. He lay on his left side for the years of Israel's punishment and on his right side for the years of Judah's punishment (4:4-8).
3. He ate meager rations to demonstrate hunger, starvation (4:9-17).
4. He cut his hair and divided it into three parts to represent the destruction and scattering of Israel (5:1-17).
5. He dug under a wall and took his baggage to portray exile (12:1-16).
6. He did not shed a tear for his wife's death, just as the Jews in exile would lose their capacity to mourn for the loss of Jerusalem and their relatives (24:15-24).

These symbolic acts, combined with Ezekiel's recorded messages, left no doubt in the minds of the Jewish faithful in exile that the Lord was prophesying doom upon Jerusalem. Contrary to their hopes of a temporary sojourn in Babylon, they were to prepare room for the new waves of exiles. Ezekiel's denunciations of the wickedness of Jerusalem's Jews was shrill and pointed. He also used allegory (especially in chapters 16 and 23) to portray their idolatry and breaking the Lord's covenants.

Many Jews in exile felt the sins of their fathers and others of their own generation were to blame for their condition (18:2). Ezekiel placed the blame upon themselves and reminded them of their personal responsibilities. (Study 3:16-21; 14:12-23; 18:1-32; and 33:1-20 to see how he espoused this important concept.)

After presenting acts and teachings of judgment upon Judah and Jerusalem in his first twenty-four chapters, Ezekiel delivers three types of messages in his last twenty-four chapters. Chapters 27-32 contain oracles against the foreign nations. Chapters 33-39 proclaim hope as Ezekiel anticipates the restoration of Israel. In the last chapters,

40-48, Ezekiel prophesies of the last days as he describes the restored temple in Jerusalem and other conditions in Israel, including the territories of the twelve tribes.

Although stern in his early pronouncements, Ezekiel also expressed hope for future Israel. Although bizarre, he was also effective in communicating the messages from the Lord. Although visionary, he was also down-to-earth as he mingled with and taught the Jews in their Babylonian exile. Although the Babylonian Jews could look to Daniel with pride because of his role with the kings, they associated on a more personal level with their own priest-prophet of the captivity, Ezekiel.

Bible Dictionary references: Ezekiel; Cherubim; Ephraim, Stick of; Judah, Stick of; Gog; Magog.

East Gate of Ezekiel's Temple
(Ezek. 40-46)

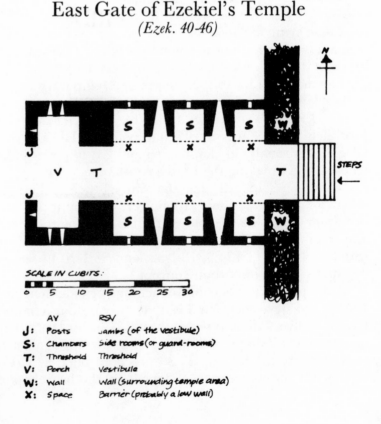

SCALE IN CUBITS:

0   5   10   15   20   25   30

	AV	RSV
J:	Posts	Jambs (of the vestibule)
S:	Chambers	Side rooms (or guard-rooms)
T:	Threshold	Threshold
V:	Porch	Vestibule
W:	Wall	Wall (surrounding temple area)
X:	Space	Barrier (probably a low wall)

Ezekiel's Temple
(Ezek. 40-46)

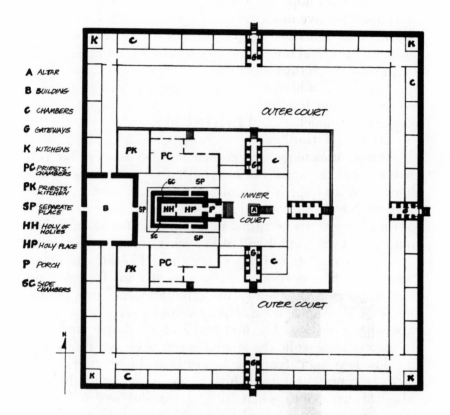

A ALTAR

B BUILDING

C CHAMBERS

G GATEWAYS

K KITCHENS

PC PRIESTS' CHAMBERS

PK PRIESTS' KITCHEN

SP SEPARATE PLACE

HH HOLY OF HOLIES

HP HOLY PLACE

P PORCH

SC SIDE CHAMBERS

Daniel

Daniel is usually well-known to LDS readers for two reasons: (1) the stories of his youth and his episode in the lion's den and (2) his prophecy about the stone (the restored Church) that would roll forth and fill the earth. Both of these events are recorded in the first half of Daniel. The material in the second half of Daniel is much less familiar.

The two halves of Daniel (1-6 and 7-12) differ in many ways. The first portion is written mostly in Aramaic and records historical events, personalities, and prophecies, while the second is in Hebrew and consists of great apocalyptic visions. The first half is clear, simple, and easy to understand, while the second is symbolic and difficult.

The four apocalyptic visions of Daniel use symbols and signs to represent ancient history and to make predictions about future events when tribulations and sorrows would give way to triumph and peace. Modern readers are not alone as they struggle to understand the symbols and signs in Daniel and how they have been or will be fulfilled. Jews and Christians over the centuries have sought different fulfillments of these visions. Daniel himself did not immediately understand the meaning of what he had heard (12:8). He was told to be patient, and that the righteous who were wise in the last days would understand.

There are many ways that the Lord has revealed the events of the last days to his ancient prophets. As the prophets and writers recorded their knowledge, some (Isaiah) used prophetic symbolism, others (Song of Solomon) made allegorical representations, and still others (Daniel, Ezekiel, John) wrote apocalyptic visions. Earlier in this book in the introduction to the Song of Solomon we saw how all three forms (Isa. 66:5-13; Song. 6:10; JST Rev. 12:1, 7) were used to describe a woman appearing as a moon and a sun in the last days. But without the key from modern revelation (D&C 109:73) we would have a difficult time understanding the meaning of any one of the three ancient descriptions of this event. If we are righteous and faithful, if we listen to the modern prophets, if we study the prophecies contained in the scriptures, and if we observe the events of our age, we can understand these ancient, symbolic writings. In many ways it is easier for us to understand them than it was for the ancient peoples. Also it has been prophesied that we would be better able to understand them. (Dan. 12:10; Isa. 11:9.)

Bible Dictionary references: Daniel; Daniel, Book of; Abomination of Desolation; Adam; Gabriel; Mene mene tekel upharsin; Messiah; Michael.

Hosea

Hosea seemed to be unlikely material for a prophet. His marriage to an immoral woman and her desertion did not provide the ideal family model for other Israelites. Rather than serving as a model, Hosea's family was a mirror that reflected the immorality, disruption, and lack of family ties then present among the Israelites. His family became a symbol of the relationship of the Lord with his chosen family, the Israelites.

The book of Hosea first develops the Hosea family relationships and then illustrates the same trends in the Lord's actions with Israel. The first three chapters relate that Hosea makes an unexpected choice of a wife with an immoral background, but they are able to start a family. The wife, Gomer, soon tires of family responsibilities and returns to her life as a harlot. Hosea keeps informed of her life, and when she is ready to return home, he is willing to buy her back, which he does with tender love and a sincere hope for an eternal relationship.

The next ten chapters show the covenant relationship between the Lord and Israel being broken by the people's wickedness. They would shortly become separated as Israel continued her wicked ways. But later, even many centuries later, the Lord would still keep in touch with Israel until some of her children were willing to return to him and be accepted in his house with all the blessings and promises of a righteous people.

The last chapter is an open invitation to Israel to return to the Lord to receive these blessings. The book could be outlined as follows:

I.   Hosea's marital experience portrays God's relationship with Israel (1-3).
    A.   Hosea marries Gomer, whose three children are a sign to Israel (1).
    B.   Gomer rejects her husband, while he waits (2).
    C.   Hosea redeems his wife from her owner (3).
II. Hosea's words of judgment to Israel (and later Judah, 4-13).
    A.   Pride, idolatry, and corruption of Israel (and Judah) (4-8).
    B.   Judgments and captivity to come upon Israel as the Lord awaits her return (9-11).
    C.   The Lord's actions with Jacob (Israel) and his redeeming powers (12-13).
III. A call to Israel to repent and be blessed (14).

Hosea is difficult to understand and translate because of the poor quality of the Hebrew text. Even the earliest copies from the Dead Sea Scrolls show signs of a sloppy Hebrew transmission of the Hosea material. In fact, the Hebrew text of Hosea is probably more corrupt than any other Old Testament book. Many of the alterations may be accidental. For example, in the Hebrew text, some letters are transposed (like spelling "strength" as "strenght" or "bale" as "able"). Also, some similar consonants are confused with each other (as in English, writing "strength" as "strenyth" or "bale" as "dale"). Compare the following footnotes in the Bible to see some of the possible changes as the text is "straightened out" or modified:

	King James Version	Footnote (alternate meaning)
4:18	with shame do love	deeply love and dishonor
5:11	commandment	filth (or vanity)
13:14	repentance	compassion

In spite of these questions about Hosea's family and the poor Hebrew text, the book of Hosea gives hope and promise to Israelites as they return to the Lord. Hosea's symbolism of a renewed marriage covenant between the Lord and Israel was later repeated by the prophets Isaiah (40, 49, 51, 54, 61, 62, 66), Jeremiah (2, 3), and Ezekiel (16, 33).

There is also a lesson from Hosea for Latter-day Saints today as they see loved ones go the way of the world. We should not lose contact with them but wait, hope, and pray for their return to the family of the Lord as his chosen children. (See BD "Hosea.")

Why Would Hosea Marry a "Wife of Whoredoms"?
(Hosea 1:2)

The most obvious answer is because the Lord told him to. But why did the Lord want a prophet to marry an immoral woman?

One could ask a similar question today as one observes a young Latter-day Saint fall in love with a person with a very sinful past. When challenged, the member could respond with "Well, he (or she) has changed and I have received a confirmation through the Spirit that I should marry this person." Such a marriage with a person with an immoral past who has demonstrated an attitude of change and repentance could merit the Lord's approbation. Hosea's wife also seemed to be genuine in her early vows and marriage as she bore their first son.

But just because two people start off a marriage well is no guarantee it will succeed. Even where both parties have been moral and faithful prior to marriage, it happens all too frequently that one partner later becomes unfaithful and rejects the marriage relationship. This was easy for Gomer to do because of her earlier immoral experiences.

As Hosea waited patiently for her eventual return, his love for Gomer continued and he developed a greater sensitivity for the love which God has for all his children, especially those who turn away from him. Hosea could not force her back to him any more than the Lord will force us back into his company. (Likewise we should maintain love and patience for our wayward family members and friends.)

Through these experiences, Hosea developed love, sensitivity, patience, and understanding. Even though the acquisition of these traits came through sorrow and grief, they helped him become a more effective prophet.

The Names of Hosea's Children
(Hosea 1:4, 6, 9)

The names of Hosea's three children are unusual. The first son was called Jezreel, meaning "God (El) plants" or "God sows," just as God planted or began the house of Israel with great potential and promises.

The second two children were possibly not fathered by Hosea, although Gomer bore them while still living with him. The reasons for this speculation are that the record says the first child, Jezreel, was born to Hosea (verse 3) while the other two were simply born to Gomer (verses 6 and 8). Also, Hosea was told by the Lord that he was to take unto himself "children of whoredoms" (verse 2), and unless there were other unnamed children that fulfilled this promise, the last two named children seem to meet these requirements, partially because of their names.

The second child was a daughter named Lo-ruhamah, meaning "no mercy" or "no pity," an unlikely name for a legitimate child. The third child, a boy, was called Lo-ammi, meaning "not my people," which could suggest an illicit parentage.

In any case these names also were a symbol to the Israelites, telling them that they had originally been planted by the Lord but that he would now show them no mercy because they were no longer his people. The names of these three children were a sign to Israel of the Lord's promises and warnings to them.

Joel

This short, powerful book warns Judah of a mighty invasion and highlights some events of the last days. In the first chapter, Joel develops a variety of poetic parallelisms as he graphically portrays the invasion. In five stanzas he speaks to different segments of the adult community and describes their reactions to the destruction. The main points of these stanzas are:

Verses	Reaction of the People	Destruction
2,3,4	Hear ye old men give ear ye inhabitants	four locust invasions are in the fields
5,6,7	Awake ye drunkards howl ye wine drinkers	an army strips the vines and the trees
8,9,10	Lament like a widowed virgin (or young woman)	for the fields are destroyed
11,12,13	Be ashamed ye farmers howl ye vinedressers	for the vines and the trees are destroyed
14-20	Get dressed and lament ye priests howl ye temple minister come in sackcloth ye public ministers	and fast and pray together with the people because of the destruction upon the whole land.

The first four stanzas describe two contrasting sets of people (old men–young women, wine drinkers–wine producers) reacting to two parallel sets of destruction (invasion and destruction of fields, invasion and destruction of orchards). These verses also present the sequence of feelings a people would probably experience in such a catastrophe: first they hear about the invasion as they awake, then they scream or cry out and weep, and finally they are ashamed and sorrowful as they realize the seriousness of the events.

The last stanza (14-20) tells the religious leaders and the people what they should do in this time of distress. They are to turn to the Lord and repent. While they fast and pray in their assemblies, they should understand that the Lord's judgments have come upon them, as they have lost both physical blessings and the Lord's spiritual companionship (16).

The second chapter of Joel continues the theme of invasion, destruction, fasting, and prayer, but seems to be more descriptive of the last days than of ancient Israel. Also, this chapter promises a time of restoration, peace, and spiritual manifestations. The last part of this chapter was quoted by Moroni to Joseph Smith, and its fulfillment is to come in this dispensation (JS-H 1:41). The second chapter has four main parts:

1. The fear of the people during an invasion (1-11).
2. The people turning to the merciful Lord (12-14); he accepts Israel as his bride (15-17).
3. The Lord responds with promises and blessings (18-27).
4. Signs in the heavens and on earth for those chosen by the Lord (28-32).

Notice the organized sequence of events:

1. Fear of the people in the face of coming destruction.
2. They turn to the Lord.
3. He blesses and protects them.
4. Joy of the people in the presence of their Lord.

Also, each of the four sets of ideas is carefully organized in a variety of parallel patterns. Following is a more detailed outline of the chapter sections (each in chiastic parallelism):

1. The Invasion (1-11).
   a. Day of the Lord comes (1). a¹. Great is the day of the
   Lord (11).
   b. Day of darkness (2).   b¹. Darkness in heavens
   (10).
   c. Fire (3).   c¹. Earthquakes (10).
   d. Running and movement   d¹. Running and move-
   of army (4-5).   ment of the army (7-9).
   e. Fear of the people (6).

2. The people join the Lord (12-17).
   a. They turn to the Lord with fasting and prayer (12).
   b. They rend their hearts and repent (13).
   c. They accept the mercy (Atonement) of the Lord
   (13).
   b¹. He forgives and blesses them (13, 14).
   a¹. They turn to the Lord with sacrifices (14).
   The Lord and Israel make a covenant (15-17).
   a. The people gather in fasting and prayer (15, 16).
   b. The bride and the groom (Israel and the Lord) go
   forth together (16).
   a¹. The people are cleansed (17).

3. The Lord blesses the people (18-27).
   a. The Lord has pity for his people (18).
   b. The Lord speaks and promises:
      1. Corn, wine, and oil (19).
      2. Satisfaction (19).
      3. Destruction of the enemy army (20).
   c. Joel responds and promises:
      1. Peace and blessing on earth (to the land, animals,
      plants, and people; 21-23).
      2. Blessings from heaven (rain; 23).
   b¹. The Lord again speaks and promises:
      1. Corn, wine, and oil (24).
      2. Satisfaction (26).
      3. Destruction of the locusts and the presence of the
      Lord's army (25).
   a¹. The Lord and his people have love and respect for
   each other (27).

4. The signs of the Lord (28-32).
   a. The Lord's spirit will come upon all people (28-29; compare 1:1-13; 2:6 for the natural man's reactions).
   b. Signs in the heavens and the earth (30-31; compare the same signs in 2:2, 10).
   a¹. Those who call upon the Lord and the remnant of Israel whom the Lord calls will be delivered (32; compare 2:13, 16, 20, 25, 27 for similar promises conditional upon the people's righteousness).

The last chapter of Joel talks more about the chosen people of the Lord, especially the remnants of Judah (the Jews), who will be gathered in the last days. This chapter is organized as follows:

A. Judah and Jerusalem shall return (1).
B. Nations of the earth are judged (with nations north and south of Judea singled out; 2-12).
   1. Nations gather to Jehoshaphat (2).
   1¹. Nations gather to Jehoshaphat (11, 12).
   2. Gentiles have power over Israel (3).
   2¹. Weak have power over the strong (9, 10).
   3. Nation to the north, Lebanon, to receive divine retribution (4).
   3¹. Nation to the south, Sheba, to receive divine retribution (8).
   4. Nations have taken money and treasures from the Lord (5).
   4¹. The Lord's people will return from lands where they were sold (7).
   5. The children of Judah have been sold to the Greeks (the Gentiles, the pagan world, the nations of apostasy; 6).
C. The harvest is full (13).
D. Multitudes (of Gentiles) in the valley of Jehoshaphat, just outside Jerusalem (14).
E. The day of the Lord is near (14).
F. The sun, moon, and stars become darkened (15).
G. The Lord will speak from Zion and from Jerusalem (16).

F¹. The heavens and earth will shake (16).

E¹. People will know the Lord of this earth (17).

D¹.No strangers (Gentiles) will be allowed inside Jerusalem (17).

C¹. Plentiful harvests (18).

B¹. Nations west and east of Judea will become desolate because of their violence against the children of Judah (19).

A¹. Judah and Jerusalem will be blessed as the Lord dwells in Zion (20-21).

As can be seen in these chapters, Joel was a skillful writer who combined many poetic forms (such as all seven forms of parallelism, rhythm, descriptive details, alliteration, etc.) into an organized message. He also incorporated many ideas (and even exact quotations, words, phrases, and terms) found in many other prophetic writings. Among the terms found in Joel and in other Old Testament passages are:

Joel	Term, phrase, or idea	Also in
1:15	Alas for the day	Ezek. 30:2
1:15	The day of the Lord is near	Isa. 13:6; Ezek. 30:3; Obad. 1:15; Zeph. 1:7
1:15	Destruction from the Almighty	Isa. 13:6
2:1	Trumpet warning judgment	Isa. 27:13; Zeph. 1:16
2:2	The day of darkness is near	Zeph. 1:14-15
2:3	Garden land becomes a desert	Isa. 51:3; Ezek. 36:35 (idea reversed)
2:6	Faces "grow pale"	Nahum 2:10; the only other place where this verb is used
2:10,31; 3:15	Darkness in last days	Isa. 13:10, 13; Ezek. 32:7
2:11	The voice and power of God	Isa. 30:30; Mal. 3:2; 4:5

2:13	Catalog of God's mercies	Ex. 34:6; Jonah 4:2
2:14	Will God return and repent?	Jonah 3:9
2:14	People asking about Israel's God	Ps. 79:10; 115:2
2:21	Rejoice in what the Lord has done	Ps. 126:3
2:27	I am your God, there is none else	Isa. 45:5, 6, 18
2:28	The Lord will pour out his Spirit	Ezek. 39:29
2:31	Great and terrible day	Mal. 4:5
2:32	Those in Mount Zion will escape	Obad. 1:17
3:1	In those days, at that time	Jer. 33:15; 50:4, 20
3:2	The Lord will gather all nations	Isa. 66:18; Zech. 14:2
3:4	The Lord will return recompense	Obad. 1:15
3:8	For the Lord has spoken	Isa. 1:2; Obad. 1:18
3:10	Swords, plowshares, pruning-hooks, spears	Isa. 2:4; Micah 4:3
3:13	Grain harvest like a judgment	Isa. 17:5
3:16	The Lord roars from Zion	Ps. 61:3; Isa. 13:13; Amos 1:2;
3:17	You will know the Lord your God	Isa. 52:1; Ezek. 36:11
3:18	Mountains dripping sweet wine	Amos 9:13
3:18	Healing waters from Jerusalem	Ezek. 47:1-12; Zech. 14:8

It is possible that Joel lived early in the eighth century B.C. and that he was later quoted by many other prophets. However, it is more likely that he lived in the fifth century B.C. and quoted and borrowed from these many earlier sources in making his own message.

In either case, Joel's ideas are found in many other biblical passages. Whether he was a source of inspiration for these writers or if he borrowed from them, his message of the last days is well founded and ought to be studied carefully. (See BD "Joel.")

The Meaning of Joel's Name
(Joel 1:1)

This name is fairly common in the Old Testament. It means "the Lord (Jehovah) is God." It borrows the "Jo" from "Jahweh" and the "El" from "Elohim." Thus, it reverses the component parts found in the name "Elijah," the "El" from "Elohim" and the "Jah" from "Jahweh."

One dozen men from the period of Samuel to the end of the Old Testament are named Joel. Very little is known about most of them, and this is particularly true about the author of this book. He gives no dates, no king's names, and very little other information about himself or where and when he lived. Since he mentions no kings among the other leaders of society in chapter one, and since he usually addresses Judah and Jerusalem with only three brief mentions of Israel (2:27; 3:2, 16), it is generally assumed that he lived in Judea after the Jews returned from Babylon. If this is true, he and Malachi were among the last of the Old Testament prophets. (See BD "El"; "God"; "Jehovah"; "Names of persons.")

Who Is This Mighty Army Invading Judah?
(Joel 2:1-11)

If Joel is continuing the ideas of chapter one, he could be describing a mighty plague of destructive locusts.

Or, if he lived in the eighth century B.C., he could be portraying either the Assyrian invasions of the eighth century or the Babylonian invasions of the sixth century B.C.

If he was among the last of the ancient Old Testament prophets, then this could be a description of the Roman destruction of Jerusalem in 70 A.D. But more likely, he is highlighting the wars of Gog and Magog that will precede the Millennium. Since the last verses of chapter two were quoted to Joseph Smith, and he was told that these prophecies were soon to be fulfilled (JS-H 1:41), it is possible that Joel was using an analogy of locusts to describe the invading forces upon Judah in the last days. See also Matthew 24, especially the corresponding Joseph Smith Translation and Bible footnotes, for further details about these events.

Amos

Amos, the "burden bearer," lived in a small village six miles south of Bethlehem where he could look down upon the Jordan Valley and the Dead Sea. As a wool producer, he probably made trips into the northern towns of Israel and saw the religious and social corruption which he strongly rebuked.

Amos apparently appreciated that people do not like to be called to repentance. Instead of beginning his work with an immediate rebuke of the Israelites (as did Isaiah, Jeremiah, Ezekiel, and Micah), Amos first addressed the neighboring nations that did not share any heritage with the descendants of Abraham. After denouncing these three foreign nations (Syria, Philistia, Phoenicia), he warned some of the other tribes descended from Abraham (and Lot) of the judgments of the Lord coming upon them. After warning Edom, Ammon, and Moab, Amos pronounced the Lord's word upon Judah and finally Israel. (See BD "Amos"; see also "History of the Palestine Area, 760-690 B.C.," on pp. 98-101 of this book.)

The third chapter of Amos is familiar to most Latter-day Saints because of the statement that the Lord reveals his word to the prophets (verse 7). This secret word of the Lord to Amos was a revelation about the wickedness of the people. Amos used this statement to answer the question, "By what authority does a prophet call a people to repentance?" Amos had outlined some examples of cause and effect relationships (verses 3-6) and concluded with the fact that if problems or judgments were coming upon a people, it would be because the Lord knew of their wickedness (JST verse 16). The Lord knew and revealed this message to the prophet Amos, who then reviewed the many ways the people merited divine judgments because of their wickedness (3-6).

The third and last section of Amos (7-9) includes five visions (locusts, 7:1-3; fire, 7:4-6; plumb line, 7:7-9; basket of ripe fruit, 8:1-3; and the Lord in the temple, 9:1-4), an account of how Amos was forbidden to testify any more in Bethel (7:10-17), prophecies of doom (8:4–9:10), and promises of a restoration, a return of some Israelites, and the Lord's blessings in the land (9:11-15).

Why Did Amaziah Confront Amos?
(Amos 7:10-17)

This short biographical segment of Amos is written in the first person, probably by the hand of Amos shortly after these events occurred. Amaziah, the apostate priest of Jeroboam II at Bethel, was alarmed by Amos's predictions. He accused Amos of conspiracy against the king and ordered him to leave, to return home to Judah, and to live and prophesy there. By telling Amos to "eat bread" (verse 12) in Judah, Amaziah was using an idiomatic expression meaning to "earn one's living," thus insinuating that Amos had assumed the role of seer for personal gain.

Amos replied that he was not a prophet by profession, but that he had been called from his pastoral livelihood by the Lord to prophesy unto Israel. As a sign of his prophetic calling, Amos denounced the false priest and predicted the doom of his family.

Obadiah

This shortest book of the Old Testament contains a pronouncement against Edom (verses 1-14) and a promise of the day of the Lord (verses 15-21). It was written after a destruction and invasion of Jerusalem in which the Edomites willingly participated (verse 11). This was probably the Babylonian invasion of 587-86 B.C., for which ample Edomite hostility was recorded. (Lam. 4:21; Ezek. 25:12-14; 35:5, 10-15; 36:5; Ps. 137:7.)

There are many similarities between the first nine verses of Obadiah and chapter 49 of Jeremiah. It is unclear if these contemporary prophets were quoting from each other (and if so, who was quoting whom) or if they both were using an earlier prophecy against Edom as the basis for their own pronouncements.

Similarly, there are many comparisons between the last half dozen verses of Obadiah with the writings of Joel. However, Joel recorded in 2:32 that he was quoting an earlier prophecy (of Obadiah in verse 17) by stating "as the Lord *has* said."

John the Revelator also built upon Obadiah's words. He amplified two phrases found in the last verses of Obadiah. The holy mountain of Zion (verses 16, 17, 21) would be reserved for those who have escaped condemnation and judgment in the events immediately preceding the Millennium. John's new Jerusalem would be a holy city for those whose names were found in the book of life and who were victorious over sin. (Rev. 21:7, 27.) Thus, Latter-day Saints can easily associate "saviors on Mount Zion" (verse 21) with such record keeping and righteousness (as demonstrated through books of remembrance and temple work).

Also the phrase "the kingdom shall be the Lord's" in verse 21 was expanded by John into the triumphal chorus: "the kingdom of the world has become the kingdom of our Lord and of his Christ." (Rev. 11:15.)

Although short, this book had a message for ancient Israel and her prophets. It also inspired Christ's beloved apostle, John. It can also edify us today as it encourages us to become saviors on Mount Zion lest we want to suffer as did the ancient Edomites; for those who are not for the Lord will be against him and his work. (See BD "Obadiah"; see also "History of the Palestine Area, 690-580 B.C.," on pages 105-8 of this book.)

Jonah

The story of Jonah is more familiar to most Bible readers than any other writing among the twelve minor
prophets. Containing mostly historical narrative and very
little prophecy, this short book reveals surprise after surprise in the attitudes and actions of an ancient Israelite
prophet.

The first surprise comes when Jonah is told to preach
repentance to a pagan nation (1:1-2). Usually the prophets
prophesied judgments to the gentiles and saved their messages of repentance to be given to Israel, but Jonah was to
go to the powerful enemy of Israel.

The second surprise is Jonah's reaction to the divine
commission—he goes in the opposite direction (1:3). Earlier prophets had lost their lives in less bold actions against
the Lord (see the story of Balaam in Num. 22-24 and
the episode of the man of God from Judah in 1 Kings
13:20-24).

Instead of the Lord striking down Jonah, he preserved
Jonah's life through a great fish he had prepared for this
purpose—a third surprise (1:17, 2:10).

The fourth surprise comes when the wicked, war-loving,
pagan Assyrians in Ninevah and its suburbs repent, and
the Lord's punishments against them are stayed (3:5-10;
see also "History of the Palestine Area," on pp. 98-101 of
this book.)

The last surprise occurs as Jonah becomes upset at the Lord's mercy and asks the Lord to take his life (4:1-3).

A reader might ask why a prophet might exhibit such attitudes and then be so honest as to record them for posterity. There have been other great religious leaders who honestly admitted earlier, serious mistakes in their lives (Paul and Alma the Younger), but with Jonah we are not told how these experiences may have affected his later life and ministry.

Even though the story of Jonah as presently recorded was possibly written by someone long after Jonah's time (see BD "Jonah"), he must have told or written his story in order for it to become so well known. Also, the prayer of chapter two was probably recorded by him shortly after the event occurred.

Many Bible critics consider the story of Jonah to be an allegory or a parable. However, Jesus said that Jonah preached repentance to Nineveh (Luke 11:29-32) and that the episode in the whale was a sign of Christ's own death and resurrection.

The four chapters of the book are neatly organized as follows:

Chapter 1: Jonah's mission to Nineveh; his disobedience and the results.

Chapter 2: Jonah's prayer to the Lord.

Chapter 3: Jonah's mission to Nineveh: his obedience and the results.

Chapter 4: The Lord's discourse to Jonah.

More than a story about Jonah, this book illustrates the love and patience of God toward a weak servant and His children outside the house of Israel.

How Was Jonah Preserved for Three Days in the Belly of a Fish?
(Jonah 1:17)

Jonah's preservation could be considered as a fortuitous series of circumstances wherein a giant sperm whale wandered outside its normal habitat into the Mediterranean

Sea and then swallowed Jonah and returned him to shore. Stories and examples of other mortals who have survived similar episodes within whales are given to illustrate the possibility of such an occurrence (for example, the story of the famous seaman, James Bartley; see W. Cleon Skousen, *The Fourth Thousand Years* [Salt Lake City: Bookcraft, 1966], pp. 458-63).

A second explanation would be simply to consider this as another of the Lord's many miracles upon the earth. The use of a fish "prepared" by the Lord to preserve and transport Jonah should be no surprise.

A third and more likely explanation of these events would be to consider how Jesus used the example of Jonah in the New Testament. Jonah's three-day period within the fish was described by Jesus as a sign of his own death and resurrection. (Matt. 12:38-41.)

The story of Alma the Younger (Alma 36) is the best scriptural comparison to the episode of Jonah. It should be carefully studied along with Jonah 2. In both cases, the Lord used divine manifestations to force a zealous but misguided child into evaluating his relationship to God. Also in both cases, these children decided to thereafter serve the Lord. It would be better if God's children would commit themselves on their own to the Lord's service. But if necessary, the Lord will cause his children to know the direction of their actions long before they come before him in a final judgment and while they still have time to correct their behavior and give the great service of which they are capable.

Micah

Micah contains many little messages assembled together without an easily recognized design.

The smaller segments of Micah are grouped into three collections found in chapters 1-2, 3-5, and 6-7. Each collection begins with an exhortation to the audience to "hear" the Lord's words (1:2; 3:1; 6:1). Micah then gives a series of judgments or warnings and finally concludes each message with a promise (2:12-13; 4:1–5:15; 7:14-20). The pattern of a warning followed by a promise is used by many other prophets. This pattern becomes the central theme of Micah as he warns that God will send judgment for Judah's sins, but promises eventual pardon and blessings.

In order to see how various smaller segments or literary units are combined into a larger message, the concluding promise (4-5) of Micah's second collection (3-5) is outlined below in greater detail. Portions of this promise were quoted by the Jews to the wise men and King Herod (Micah 5:2 in Matt. 2:5-6) and by Christ to the assembled Nephites and Lamanites (Micah 4:12-13 and 5:8-15 in 3 Ne. 20:15-20; 21:12-31.) Notice how in each literary unit there is often a combination of parallelisms. Read the verses and particularly try to match up the similar parts (A with A^1, B with B^1, etc.). Study each segment as a separate lesson or message and combine them to better appreciate the variety of the promises given to Israel.

Micah's words later helped preserve Jeremiah's life, as the elders of Judah quoted his warnings of 3:12. (Jer. 26:18.) Jesus also quoted Micah 7:6. (Matt. 10:35-36.)

First read this book for an overall impression. Then watch for key words and phrases, especially if they are repeated. Study the smaller segments, messages, and individual verses and appreciate their subtle meanings and poetic patterns. Finally, organize the separate elements back into a general theme or message and see how your understanding of the whole book (or chapter) has been enriched by a deeper knowledge of the component parts. Each time you come back to that portion of the scriptures, you will be able to glean new insights and meaning from the passages as your own spiritual level increases. Thus, the scriptures can be an always new source of inspiration and direction. Even in a short book such as Micah, great richness is available. (See BD "Micah.")

Micah 4-5
Detailed Outline

I.   The temple of the Lord's house (4:1-5).
    A.   People will go up to the Lord's house in the top of mountains (4:1-2).
    B.   World at peace (4:3-4).
    C.   All people will walk in God's name (4:5).

II. The Lord will gather Israelite groups (4:6-7).
    A.   The "halted" becomes a "remnant" (Lamanites?).
    B.   Those cast out become a strong nation (ten tribes?).
    C.   The afflicted to be gathered (Jews?).

III. Blessings of Bethlehem (house of David) (4:8–5:4).
    A.   And then, the "tower of Edar" (from the Hebrew, only mentioned one other time in the Old Testa-

ment; see Genesis 35:21; near Bethlehem);
your former glory will come (4:8).

B. Now the daughter labors and travails
But she will fail and be scattered to Babylon
(4:9-10).

C. And now (or, then) nations will come against you,
But you will be gathered and strengthened (4:11-13).

D. Now the daughter is besieged and
Your judge (the Lord) is humiliated (5:1).

A¹. And then, Bethlehem Ephratah,
Your formerly prophesied leader will come (5:2).

B¹. He will leave Israel scattered
Until she delivers. (5:3).

C¹. Then some of his brethren (missionaries?) will return
To the children of Israel (5:3).

D¹. He (the judge) will protect and
His glory will be great (5:4).

IV. The judge and his forces (5:5-6).
A. He will provide peace when
The Assyrians come into our land and
Tread in our palaces (5:5a).

A¹. He will deliver us when
The Assyrian comes in the land and
Treads within our borders (5:6b).

B. Seven shepherds and eight men (i.e., many leaders) will destroy Assyria (5:5b, 6a).

V. Power of the remnants of Jacob (5:7-15).
A. Remnant of Jacob
In the midst of the people as
Dew (soft) and as
showers (hard)
That come on their own (no one starts them)
(5:7).

A¹. Remnant of Jacob
     Among the Gentiles as
         him in the forest (usual setting)
             Young lion among flocks (drastic setting)
     Who strikes in power (no one can stop him) (5:8).

B.   God's hand against the adversaries and
         Enemies to be cut off (5:9).
     1. Military equipment cut off (5:10).
     2. Cities cut off (5:11).
     3. Wicked leaders cut off (5:12).
     4. Idols cut off (5:13).
         Enemies* destroyed (5:14).
     God's vengeance upon the heathen nations (5:15).

Note: Many of these sets of parallelism are much stronger and clearer in the original Hebrew text because of similar sounds and word roots. For example, in section III, items A, B, C, D, and A¹ all begin with the same sound, which is spelled two different ways (like "bow" and "bough" in English) with two different meanings. Other plays on sounds and words help identify the sets and their parallels.

Who Is the "Remnant of Israel"?
(Micah 2:12)

The term "remnant of Israel" or "remnant of Jacob" almost always refers to the descendants of Jacob who settled in America—that is, the Book of Mormon community of Lehi. These descendants are so identified in the Book of Mormon by Nephi (2 Ne. 28:2), Christ (3 Ne. 20:16), Mormon (Morm. 7:10), and Moroni (Book of Mormon title page).

This "remnant of Israel" should not be confused with

---

*This is a correct translation, since the words "city" and "enemy" come from the same Hebrew root. The term "enemies" is used here in some other English translations and makes a better parallelism. See 1 Samuel 28:16 and Psalm 139:22 for similar translations of the word.

the "remnant of Judah" (Isa. 37:31-32; Jer. 40:11, 15), which would be the Jews. Sometimes a "remnant" (without a modifying phrase) could refer to the descendants of the northern tribes preserved or returning from the Assyrian captivity (2 Chr. 30:6; Isa. 11:11, 16); or it could refer to those returning in the last days from Judah (Micah 5:3; Ezek. 6:8); or it could refer to both groups (Jer. 23:3; Isa. 1:9).

While reading the scriptures (particularly the prophetic portions), whenever you come upon the term "remnant" you should see if this term is defined or modified (remnant "of Israel" or "of Judah," etc.) in order to understand which group of Israelites is being discussed. If no modifiers are present, study the term in its context to see if it applies to any or all groups of Israelites in the last days.

Joseph Fielding Smith made the following statement about the remnants of Israel:

The remnant of the house of Israel spoken of in First Nephi, chapter 13, and Third Nephi, chapters 16, 20, and 21, does not have reference only to the descendants of Lehi, but to *all* the house of Israel, the children of Jacob, those upon *this land* and those in *other lands*. . . . Remember that all through the Lord has been speaking of the remnant of Jacob or Israel, and of the great promises made to the gentiles who are on *this land* and in *all other lands*, if they will only come into the Church and be numbered with the house of Israel. Their privileges would be to assist in building the New Jerusalem, and if they refuse, then shall the punishments come upon them. (DS 2:248, 250.)

Nahum

Most Old Testament prophets, after pronouncing warnings and judgments upon their contemporary audiences, would look to future times and events, especially the last days. Nahum reversed this order by speaking of the events at the Second Coming (chapter 1) and then warning Nineveh of her impending destruction.

Nahum prophesied to Nineveh about one hundred and fifty years after Jonah had preached to the city (see "History of the Palestine Area," on pages 105-8 of this book to compare the historical periods of Jonah and Nahum). When Jonah had called Nineveh to repentance, she was ruled by politically weak kings between periods of imperialistic power. In Nahum's time, Assyria was steadily growing weaker, and Nineveh was no longer the capital. (See BD "Nineveh.") Threatened by the Medes and Persians in the east, Babylon in the south, and mountain tribes in the north, Assyria lacked the strong leadership needed to preserve its empire. (See BD "Assyria," p. 616.) Nahum foresaw the coming destruction, and probably prophesied toward the end of the period from 663 B.C. (when Thebes or "No-Amon" fell; 3:8) to 608 B.C. (when Nineveh was razed to the ground following its destruction in 612 B.C.).

Nahum's poetic strength and beauty excelled almost all other Old Testament writers. He skillfully portrays both a God of vengeance and justice (1:2) and a God of tender compassion (1:7). Nahum recognized that God was slow to anger, but that he would surely pour out his wrath upon Nineveh (or any similar society) who opposed the Lord and oppressed his people. On the other hand, those who would take refuge in the Lord would have nothing to fear.

Nahum demonstrated God's justice in Nineveh's overthrow. He also predicted the fall of every "Nineveh" which sought to destroy God's people. Accordingly, his prophecy should be studied together with Revelation 17, John's prediction of the downfall of "Babylon." (See BD "Nahum.")

Habakkuk

Habakkuk observed the injustices in the Israelite society of his time. He questioned the Lord as to why the wicked had power over the righteous and were able to avoid fair judgments (1:1-4). The Lord answered by telling Habakkuk that he was going to raise up the Chaldeans (Babylonians) against Israel (1:5-11). Habakkuk then wondered why the Lord would use such a wicked, pagan society to punish the House of Israel, and he awaited the Lord's response (1:12–2:1). God admonished Habakkuk (and the righteous among Israel) to have patience and faith in the Lord (2:2-4). The Chaldeans would also be punished and five woes or transgressions were pronounced upon them: plundering (2:5-8), selfishness (2:9-11), oppression (2:12-14), drunken behavior (2:15-17), and idolatry (2:18-20). Indeed, all sinners would be punished, but the righteous would be preserved and receive power and blessings from the Lord through their faith (2:4, 14, 20). Habakkuk concluded his short book with a prayer that he composed as a psalm or hymn (3:1-19).

The lyric poem of chapter three describes a revelation of God coming in majesty, bringing judgment upon the pagans and blessings to his chosen children. It shifts from the first person (Habakkuk speaking) to the third person (Habakkuk describing the Lord) to the second person (Habakkuk talking to God) and back to the first person (Habakkuk giving praises). It is outlined as follows:

1. Habakkuk's confession of faith (3:2).
2. God's approach from the south (3:3-7).
3. The Lord's battle (3:8-15).
4. Habakkuk's response (3:16-19).

The major message of Habakkuk emphasizes the faith that the righteous should maintain in the face of adversity. This idea inspired the Qumran community, as recorded in their commentary on Habakkuk found among the Dead Sea Scrolls. Habakkuk's motto of faith (2:4) was also later quoted by Paul as he sought to strengthen the early Christians (Rom. 1:17; Gal. 3:11; Heb. 10:38). It can still inspire the righteous as they patiently wait for the Lord to bring judgment, rather than seeking their own justice. (See BD "Habakkuk.")

Zephaniah

Zephaniah descended from the royal family of King
Hezekiah and was a second cousin (one generation removed) from King Josiah, during whose reign he
prophesied (1:1). Zephaniah lived in Jerusalem and may
have been trained by the same teachers who influenced
Josiah toward his religous reforms. Zephaniah's message
was probably delivered before Josiah began his extensive
reformation in 622 B.C. Even if he preached during the
reformation, the Jewish masses did not respond, and Judah
was rapidly approaching her day of judgment.

Zephaniah followed the pattern of most of the Old
Testament prophets by organizing his material into three
parts: judgments to Judah (1), judgments to other nations
(2), and latter-day judgments and blessings for Israel (3).
He borrowed ideas from earlier prophets, including the
concept of the Day of the Lord (Amos 5:18; Isa. 2:7), the
faithful remnant that would encourage a religious community in the last days (Isa. 11:11-16; 37:4-32; 46:3), the eradi-
cation of hostile nations (Amos 1, 2), and the rehabilitation
of Israel by the Lord (Hosea 3, 6, 14).

For those on the earth who now await the "great day of
the Lord" (1:14) or his "great and dreadful day" (Mal.
4:5), there is a voice of warning in Zephaniah and the other
prophets. We are warned to be prepared for the judgments
that will come upon the earth and her inhabitants. But

there is also a voice of promise in these writings as we anticipate the great signs and powers of the Lord. To those who are wicked and unprepared it will be a "dreadful" day, but to those who are faithful and ready it will be a "great" day of the Lord. (See BD "Zephaniah.")

What Will Be the "Pure Language" after the Messiah's Second Coming?
(Zeph. 3:9)

One usually assumes it to be the undefiled language spoken by Adam. (See Moses 6:6.) From the early names in Genesis and those few names of the Jaredite community, it appears to be closely related to Hebrew and the other Semitic languages, but still a separate, distinct language. Perhaps a study of Hebrew, Arabic, or some other Semitic languages would help a person adjust to this millennial language.

However, a second meaning of a "pure language" is even easier for persons to work on before Christ returns. We can develop a "purified language" devoid of blasphemies, filthiness, and inappropriate terms. All our words should be clean and worthy of the Lord's ears at any time, whether he is on the earth or not. By purifying our own language today, we will be better prepared for the language of God, Adam, and the Millennium.

Haggai

Haggai is often called the "temple prophet" because of his admonition to rebuild the Lord's house in Jerusalem. Haggai received four messages or commissions from the Lord that are recorded in his brief book of thirty-eight verses.

The first message challenged the Jews to rebuild their temple (1:1-15). This message was dated in the fall of 520 B.C. It had been over sixteen years since about fifty thousand Jews had returned from Babylonia to Judea. They had quickly built an altar for sacrifices and had laid the foundation for a temple, but the temple work had been set aside because of Samaritan opposition and because the people became involved in their own homes and fields. However, the fields were not fully productive, and the people waited for a better opportunity to finish the temple. In his first message, Haggai told the Jews the land was cursed because they lacked spirituality. If they would put the temple first, their fields would be blessed. They quickly responded and resumed the temple construction within a few weeks (review Ezra 1-6 for further details concerning these events).

The second message of Haggai was to encourage the people in the temple project (2:1-9). They did not have the resources to build a magnificent temple like Solomon's, yet they were promised God's glory and presence if they completed and respected their temple.

Haggai's third message from the Lord evaluated the situation of ritual impurity among the people (2:10-19). As an unclean object rendered objects and people unclean, so would impure Israelites contaminate the temple. Physical blessings were promised them if they would honor the temple.

The fourth message of Haggai was messianic. It promised the blessings of David's throne to Zerubbabel, the Jewish governor of Judea and grandson of King Jehoichin (compare Zech. 6:11-13, where another prophet used the crowning of Joshua, the high priest of this time period, as a symbolic representation of the Messiah). Both Jehoichin (also called Jeconiah) and Zerubbabel were among Christ's ancestry. (See Matt. 1:12.)

Haggai's messages were well received by the people. This was one of the few times when the Israelites responded positively to a prophet's voice. Similar blessings and promises apply to people today if they will heed the voice of the modern prophets. (See BD "Haggai.")

Zechariah

With its fourteen chapters and 211 verses, Zechariah is the largest book among the twelve "minor" prophets (Hosea through Malachi). With visions, symbolic messianic prophecies, judgments upon nations, and signs of the last days, Zechariah is the most detailed book of the prophets who spoke after the Babylonian captivity.

Zechariah is an important book for Latter-day Saints for three reasons. First, Zechariah prophesied after the return from Babylonia. He began his prophetic service shortly after Haggai in 520 B.C. (Earlier he had served as a priest at the altar.) Since he prophesied after the Babylonian exile, his prophecies of a scattering and gathering of Israel (especially the Jews) were to be fulfilled in later times. One problem with understanding many Old Testament prophets was that when they foretold a scattering and gathering of the Jews, one cannot be sure if they were talking about the Babylonian captivity in the sixth century B.C. or the dispersion after the Roman destruction of Jerusalem in A.D. 70. With Zechariah, this ambiguity is removed, as he only refers to the later events.

A second reason for the significance of his writings is that there are more prophecies about Christ in his book than in any other prophetic book except Isaiah. These are listed here with at least one other biblical reference to the same prophecy:

Zechariah	Prophecy or Sign of Christ	*Fulfillment
1:11;	Return to Zion	Rev. 11:15;
14:5, 9		21:27
3:8	The servant	Mark 10:45
3:8;	The branch	Rom. 15:12;
6:12		Rev. 22:16
6:13	Priest—king	Heb. 6:20-7:1
9:9-10	Riding a donkey	Matt. 21:4-5;
		John 12:14-15
9:11	Atonement	Luke 22:19, 44
9:11	Work in the spirit world	1 Pet. 3:19; 4:6
10:4	The cornerstone	Matt. 21:42
11:12-13	Betrayal	Matt. 27:9-10
12:10	Hands pierced	John 19:37
13:1	Cleansing waters	Rev. 1:5
13:7	Persecution	John 8:40
13:7	Smitten shepherd	Matt. 26:31; Mark 14:27
13:9	Lord's people	Rom. 9:25
14:4	On the Mount of Olives	D&C 45:48; Acts 1:11
14:5	Resurrected Saints return with Christ	1 Thes. 4:14
14:9	King of the earth	Rev. 11:15

A third reason why Zechariah is important to Latter-day Saints is because of his many other prophecies of the last days. The Bible footnotes highlight and cross-reference these prophecies.

Zechariah's writings are difficult to understand. If one will carefully study Zechariah and ponder and pray, greater understanding and appreciation of his words will come to him. As suggested by his name, Zechariah (the Lord remembers), God has remembered his children

---

*Also see the Topical Guide references listed for these verses to find many other scriptures on these topics.

through the ages, and the Lord of this earth will return and personally rule as Lord of Lords and King of Kings.

Bible Dictionary references: Armageddon; Zechariah.

Malachi

Among the twelve books of the minor prophets, Malachi is probably the favorite among Latter-day Saints. They are especially familiar with the last two chapters (3-4) because they were quoted by Christ in the Book of Mormon (3 Ne. 24-25) and by Moroni to Joseph Smith (JS-H 41:36-39). They also identify with the teachings on tithing (3:8-12), a book of remembrance (3:16-18), and the coming of Elijah to turn the hearts of parents and children to each other (4:5-6).

Malachi spoke to the Jews during a period of religious decline. Seventy years after the spiritual emphasis of Haggai and Zechariah, the people were neglecting their religious duties and criticizing God for their problems. The appointment of a zealous Jewish governor, Nehemiah, had recently resulted in the rebuilding of Jerusalem's walls and the institution of some religious reforms (compare Neh. 7-13 for more details on the religious problems of the period). But the people were discouraged and disappointed. Malachi came to them as a messenger of hope. He promised them immediate blessings if they properly served the Lord and a future glory after the Lord had purged the wicked from the earth in his great and dreadful day.

The people wanted the blessings without having to reform themselves. They criticized Malachi's accusations and doubted whether God would ever show his power.

These attitudes were demonstrated in a repeated rhetorical pattern of teaching that Malachi had to use with the people. It involved three steps, as seen in Malachi 3:8:

1. *Accusation* by the Lord through Malachi: "You have robbed me!"
2. *Question* by the people in their defense: "Wherein have we robbed thee?"
3. *Answer* by Malachi proving their guilt: "In tithes and offerings."

The key element in this pattern was the phrase "And (yet, but) ye say . . . ," which would introduce the question or statement by which the Jews tried to defend or justify themselves. This phrase was repeated eight times in Malachi's short book: 1:2, 6, 7; 2:14, 17; 3:7, 8, 13.

The book of Malachi can be divided into seven main sections. In each of the first six sections, Malachi addresses a particular unrighteous group and their problems. He usually gives them some hope or promises them a blessing if they will correct their weakness. These sections are outlined as follows:

Verses	Problem	Promise
1:2-5	People questioning God's love.	God will destroy Edom (the wicked).
1:6-2:9	Sins of the priests.	Covenant of peace with the Levites.
2:10-16	Adultery and idolatry.	God wants a godly people.
2:17-3:6	Doubting God's justice.	God will be pleased with Judah (after a purging).
3:7-12	Withholding tithes, offerings (sins of the people).	Windows of heaven will be opened.
3:13-18	Sceptics wonder why they should keep the commandments.	Righteous people will be God's jewels.

The last section (and chapter) of Malachi talks about

the coming great and dreadful day of the Lord. It is organized into a weak chiastic pattern:

(a) The day of the Lord is coming; the wicked will be burned as stubble (1).

(b) Those who fear (revere) the Lord will have power over the wicked (2, 3).

(c) Remember (and keep) the laws and the commandments (4).

(b^1) Those parents and children who remember each other will be preserved (5, 6).

(a^1) The great and dreadful day of the Lord is coming; the earth will almost be destroyed (5, 6).

Malachi was the last of the Old Testament prophets, literally and symbolically. Between his ministry (about 450-430 B.C.) and the time of the New Testament there were no prophets among the Jews. Indeed, the Jews still consider Malachi as their last prophet, since they do not accept the prophets and apostles of Jesus or the living prophets of today.

Symbolically Malachi was the last prophet to a dispensation that began with a great prophet, Moses, and many miracles and teachings. But a thousand years later the people were still slaves, not to Egypt, but to worldliness, pride, and their physical appetites. What good had the centuries of preaching, teaching, and prophesying done for the Israelites? Only a few of them followed the Lord. As Malachi reviewed their sins and problems, he warned them of the Lord's final judgments and refining fires. There would come a time when the wicked would be consumed and the Lord would finally rule over his children on a world of righteousness. Malachi's witness of this coming judgment and day of the Lord is an appropriate conclusion to the witness of the Old Testament. (See BD "Malachi.")

Bibliography

Clark, James R., comp. *Messages of the First Presidency of The Church of Jesus Christ of Latter-day Saints.* 6 vols. Salt Lake City: Bookcraft, 1965-75.

Hunter, Milton R. *Pearl of Great Price Commentary.* Salt Lake City: Bookcraft, 1959.

Journal of Discourses. 26 vols. London: Latter-day Saints' Book Depot, 1854-86.

Kimball, Spencer W. *Faith Precedes the Miracle.* Salt Lake City: Deseret Book Company, 1972.

McConkie, Bruce R. *Mormon Doctrine.* 2nd ed. Salt Lake City: Bookcraft, 1966.

Smith, Joseph. *History of The Church of Jesus Christ of Latter-day Saints.* 7 vols. 2nd ed. rev. Edited by B. H. Roberts. Salt Lake City: The Church of Jesus Christ of Latter-day Saints, 1932-51.

————. *Teachings of the Prophet Joseph Smith.* Selected by Joseph Fielding Smith. Salt Lake City: Deseret Book Company, 1938.

Smith, Joseph Fielding. *Answers to Gospel Questions.* 5 vols. Compiled by Joseph Fielding Smith, Jr. Salt Lake City: Deseret Book Company, 1957-66.

————. *Doctrines of Salvation.* 3 vols. Compiled by Bruce R. McConkie. Salt Lake City: Bookcraft, 1954-56.

————. *Man: His Origin and Destiny.* Salt Lake City: Deseret Book Company, 1954.

Talmage, James E. *The Articles of Faith.* 12th ed. Salt Lake City: The Church of Jesus Christ of Latter-day Saints, 1924.

Index

Abimelech, 13, 15-16
Abraham: dispensation of, 3; vision of, 5; chronology of, 11-13; travels of, 13; received birthright blessing, 17
Acrostic poetic form, 137
Adam: dispensation of, 3; created or born, 6; deaths of, 7-8
Adamic language, 225
Amos: overview of, 208; judgments of, 208-9; Amaziah's confrontation with, 209
Animals on ark, 10
Army, mighty, invading Judah, 206-7
Ascents, songs of, 137
Ashtart, 66-67
Assyrian: invasions, 102; provinces, 103

Baal, 66-67
Balaam, 48-49
Baptism, 15, 31
Birthright inheritance and blessing, 16-17
Blessing, birthright, 16-17
Blood, eating of, 11
Books of the Law, 22
Burden of offender, 38-39
Burnt offering, 34

Cain's offering, 8
Camp of Israel, 46

Canaan, conquest of, 60
Census figures, 43-45
Chiasmus, 173, 233
Childs, Brevard S., 86
Chronicles: overview of books of, 110-12
Circumcision, 15
Cities of refuge, 60-61
City-states, five, 13-14
"Clean" animals, 10
Cockatrice, 174
Collection of books, O.T. is a, 1-2
Covenant people, 168
Covenants, 52-53
Creation, "days" of, 4-6

Daniel: overview of, 194-95; Bible Dictionary references for, 195
David: runs from Saul, 80; wars of, 81; authored some psalms, 126-27
Day of Atonement, 32-33, 35-36, 37
"Days" of creation, 4-6
Deborah, 68-69
Degrees, songs of, 137
Delilah, 72-73
Deuteronomy: overview of, 51-53; Bible Dictionary references for, 53
Dietary laws, 28
Divided kingdoms, 92-94
Dividing of earth, 11
Drink offering, 36

Earth: baptism of, 9; dividing of, 11; heaven is above, 172-73

Ebla, 14

Ecclesiastes, overview of, 140-41

Edom, 174-75, 210

Elihu's tirade, 121-22

Elijah's travels, 95-96

Elisha's power, 97-98

Enmity, 8

Enoch, dispensation of, 3

Ephraim, received birthright blessing, 17

Esther, overview of, 117

Eve, creation of, 7

Exodus: overview of, 22; Bible Dictionary references for, 23

Eye-for-an-eye punishment, 39

Ezekiel: overview of, 190-92; Bible Dictionary references for, 192; temple of, 192-93

Ezra and Nehemiah: overview of books of, 114-15; Bible Dictionary references for, 115

Feast of Weeks, 36

Festivals, 28

Fishers and hunters among Israelites, 181-82

Five city-states, 13-14

Flood, 8-10

Foreign nations, Isaiah's prophecies to, 160-61

Gathering of Jews, 182-86

Genealogy of Moses, 26

Genesis: overview of, 3-4; Bible Dictionary references for, 4

Gentle waters vs. flood, 154

Guilt offering, 36

Habakkuk, overview of, 222-23

Hagar, 13-14

Haggai, overview of, 226-27

Hand under thigh, 16

Haran, 12

Heave offering, 36-37

Heavenly Father, feeling close to, 173-74

Heavens: as a scroll, 163-64; above earth, 172-73

Hebrew letters in Psalm 119, 137

Hezekiah: the Jerusalem of, 164; problems of, 165-66

High priest, robes of, 30

Hosea: overview of, 196-98; marries immoral wife, 198-99; names of children of, 199

Hunters and fishers among Israelites, 181-82

Inheritance, birthright, 16-17

Instructions and promises from the Lord, 162-63

"In that day," 149

Invasion toward Jerusalem, 154

Isaac: generation of, 3; in Abraham's chronology, 13; received birthright blessing, 17

Isaiah: overview of book of, 145-48; summary of writings of, 147-48; preface of, 148-49; difficulty of understanding, 150-52; strange names of sons of, 153-54; importance of eleventh chapter of, 155-60; message of chapter 29, 163; hopes of, 172; mixes good and bad news together, 175-76

Ishmael, 13

Israel: promises for, 152-53; Syria and, against Judah, 153; speaking to, 167-68

Jacob: generation of, 3; received birthright blessing, 17; gave blessings, 18

Jephthah, 69-70

Jeremiah: overview of, 177-81; of particular interest to Mormons, 179; prophecies on gathering, 182-86

Jericho, walls of, 56-57
Jesus Christ, as Messiah, 169-71
Jews, gathering of, 182-86
Job: overview of, 118-24; five parts
   of book, 119; prose prologue of,
   119-20; poetic dialogue with
   friends of, 120-21; Elihu's tirade,
   121-22; Lord's answers to, 122-
   23; prose epilogue of, 123-24;
   questions raised in, 123-24;
   time period of, 124
Joel: overview of, 200-206;
   meaning of name of, 206
John the Baptist, 47
Jonah: overview of, 212-13; in the
   whale, 213-14
Joseph: generation of, 3; received
   birthright blessing, 17; blessings
   of, 18; prophecies of, 19-21
Joshua: overview of, 54-55; Bible
   Dictionary references for, 55;
   campaigns of, 57-59
Josiah: expanded kingdom of, 112;
   futile battle of, 113
Judah: blessings of, 18; last kings
   of, 109; after return from
   Babylon, 116; waters of, 168;
   mighty army invading, 206-7
Judges: overview of, 62-66; twelve,
   64-65; Bible Dictionary
   references for, 66
Justice: under law of Moses, 38-40;
   law of, 169-71

Kolob, 5
Keturah, 13
Kimball, Spencer W.: on abiding
   God's presence, 23-24; on Ten
   Commandments, 26-27
Kings: overview of books of, 82-87;
   Bible Dictionary references for,
   87; last, of Judah, 109

Lamentations: overview of, 187;
   modern translation of part of,
   187-88
Last days, gathering of Jews in,
   182-86

Law: "of Sarah," 14-15; of Moses,
   27-28, 38-40; of justice, 169-71;
   of mercy, 170-71
Laws of purification, 28
Levitical priesthood, 29, 37-38
Leviticus: overview of, 32-33;
   Bible Dictionary references for,
   33
Library, ancient, O.T. is, 2
Lord of this earth, 166-67
Lot, 12-13

Malachi: overview of, 231-33; book
   of, favorite among Latter-day
   Saints, 231; divided into seven
   sections, 232-33
Marry us, our sons, 174
McConkie, Bruce R.: on Eve's
   creation, 7; on Balaam, 49
Meal offering, 34-35
Meat, eating of, 10-11
Melchizedek, 13
Mercy, law of, 170-71
Messiah: atonement of, 169-71;
   dialogue of, in Isaiah 63, 174
Micah: overview of, 215-16;
   outline of chapters 4 and 5,
   216-18
Middle East, peace in, 161
Mighty army invading Judah, 206-7
Moses: wrote Genesis, 3; showed
   God's work, 4; abides God's
   presence, 23-24; why chosen
   by Lord, 24; genealogy of, 25;
   law of, 27; Transjordan
   campaign of, 48
Musical instruments, 136

Nahum, overview of, 220-21
Naomi, 74-75
Nazarites, 47, 71
Nehemiah and Ezra: overview of
   books of, 114-15; Bible
   Dictionary references for, 115
Nibley, Hugh, on raising hands
   in prayer, 189
Noah: dispensation of, 3; took

seven pair of "clean" animals,
10; not commanded to eat meat,
10-11
Numbers: overview of, 41-42;
Bible Dictionary references
for, 42-43

Obadiah, overview of, 210-11
Offerings, Israelites', 34-37
Old Testament, is ancient library,
1-2

Palestine area, history of, 98-101,
105-8
Parallelism in O.T.: in Hebrew
poetry, 127-28; synonymous,
128; antithetic, 129; emblematic,
129-30; synthetic, 130;
composite, 131; climactic,
131-33; introverted, 133-35; in
Joel, 204; in Micah, 215, 218
Peace in Middle East, 161
Peace offering, 35
Pentateuch, 22
Philistines, 70-71
Pieces of silver, 72-73
Plural marriage, 14-15
Poetic forms, in Joel, 204
Poetry in O.T., understanding, 135
Prayer, raising hands in, 189
Priests, washing of, 31
Promises and instructions from
the Lord, 162-63
Prophecies: by prophets, Solomon
to Elijah, 88-92; to foreign
nations, 160-61; about Christ,
228-29
Prophetic past tense, 167
Prophets and prophecies, Solomon
to Elijah, 88-92
Prophet's message, study of, 78-79
Proverbs, overview of, 138-39
Psalm 119, Hebrew letters in, 137
Psalms: overview of, 125-26;
Bible Dictionary references for,
126; authorship of, 126-27;
songs of degrees, 137

Pure language, 225
Purification laws, 28, 32
Purim, festival of, 117

Rahab the harlot, 55-56
Raising hands in prayer, 189
Rebekah, 13
Refuge, six cities of, 60-61
Remnant of Israel, 218-19
"Reverse tithing," 149
Rights of victim, 38
Robes of Levitical priesthood, 29-30
Ruth, overview of, 74-75

Sacrifice, 27, 32
Samson, 47, 71-72
Samuel: was Nazarite, 47;
overview of books of, 76-78;
Bible Dictionary references
for, 78
Sarai (Sarah), 12-13; 14-15
Scroll, heavens as a, 163-64
Selah, 136
Sennacherib's attack, 104
Servant songs, 168-69
Seven, importance of that number,
10
Shem, received birthright blessing,
17
Silver, pieces of, 72-73
Sin offering, 35-36
Smith, Joseph, 6
Smith, Joseph Fielding: on Adam,
6-7; on eating meat, 10-11; on
eating of blood, 11; on remnants
of Israel, 219
Sodom and Gomorrah, 14
Solomon, song of, 142-44
Sons marry us, 174
Speaking to Israel, 167
Stone as witness, 61
Syria and Israel against Judah, 153

Tabernacle, illustration of, 28
Taylor, John: on the flood, 9-10;

on dividing of earth, 11
Temple, Ezekiel's, 192-93
Ten Commandments, 25-27
Terah, 12
Thank offering, 35
Theophany, 25
Thigh, hand under, 16
Tithing, 27
Torah, 22, 53
Trespass offering, 36

Urim and Thummim, 12, 29, 37, 61
Uzziah's society, 152

Vassal treaties, 51
Vows, 50

Waters of Judah, 168
Wave offering, 36-37
Witness, stone as, 61
Woman: creation of, 7; reproach of, 149; in travail, 162
World, judgment of, 162

Young, Brigham, on creation of man, 6

Zechariah: overview of, 228-30; Bible Dictionary references for, 230
Zephaniah, overview of, 224-25